EURO

The essential guide to the
European Championships

PHILIP EVANS has drafted pieces about football for
newspapers (*The Observer*, *The Sunday Times*, the *Financial
Times*, *The Scotsman*), as well as a column for the monthly
magazine *World Soccer*. He has written books before the
World Cups of 1974, 1978, 1982, 1986 and 1990, and
several quiz books about football. He is also the author of
highly-praised thrillers and short stories.

For Adam and Chris

ACKNOWLEDGEMENTS

I'm most grateful to the following for their help and advice: Brian Glanville, Martin Corey at Wembley, Ernest Hecht, Brian Moore, John Moynihan, Roberto Cianfanelli in Florence, Gerry Foley, John Gill, Tim Gutch, Robert Lipscomb in Paris, Dino Lanati in Milan, Keith Niemeyer, Roger Pring of the Cooper Dale Partnership, Anthony Shillington and Il Conte Antonio Trapani di Montpeliano. Finally to Anne Clark for asking me to write the book, and last but by no means least Beverley Birch for overseeing the project with an extremely wise eye.

EURO 96

The essential guide to the European Championships

PHILIP EVANS

Hodder
Children's
Books

a division of Hodder Headline plc

Copyright © Philip Evans 1996

The right of Philip Evans to be identified as the author of the work has been asserted by
him in accordance with the Copyright, Designs and Patents Act 1988

Published by Hodder Children's Books 1996

10 9 8 7 6 5 4 3 2 1
All rights reserved. No part of this publication may be reproduced, stored in a retrieval
system, or transmitted, in any form or by any means, without the prior written
permission of the publisher, nor be otherwise circulated in any form of binding or cover
other than that in which it is published and without a similar condition being imposed
on the subsequent purchaser.

ISBN 0340 64058 8

Hodder Children's Books
a Division of Hodder Headline plc
338 Euston Road
London NW1 3BH

Book and cover design by Christopher Halls

Printed and bound by Cox & Wyman Ltd, Reading, Berks
A Catalogue record for this book is available from the British Library

CONTENTS

INTRODUCTION 6

COUNT-DOWN TO THE FINAL 8

SURPRISES IN THE QUALIFYING COMPETITION 12

THE COMPETING COUNTRIES 16

SOME OF THE LEADING STARS 48

STATISTICS AND CURIOSITIES 68

PREVIOUS TOURNAMENTS 72

INDEX 96

INTRODUCTION

The draw for the 47 countries in the preliminary eight groups was made in Manchester on 22 January 1994, into seven groups of six countries, one of five. ENGLAND (as hosts) were excluded, but not DENMARK (as holders). During US 94 the rule that awards three points for a victory successfully encouraged attacking play. As a result that idea was also used in the European Championships.

The finals of the competition have been expanded yet again. From 1960 to 1976 the final stages had four teams. From 1980 to 1992 they comprised eight teams. Now they've been expanded to include sixteen teams.

Fifteen of these have come from the eight qualifying groups. With ENGLAND as the host country gaining automatic admission, the two worst-qualified teams played a decider to see who would go through. In this closely-fought game played at Liverpool on 13 December 1995, HOLLAND beat the REPUBLIC OF IRELAND 2-0.

Significant was the break-up of Eastern Europe, which led to fifteen teams entering for the first time. In 1992, Eastern Europe's only qualifier was the CONFEDERATION OF INDEPENDENT STATES (CIS). This time, however, there will be no less than six: BULGARIA, CROATIA, the CZECH REPUBLIC, RUMANIA, RUSSIA and TURKEY. Many of their players have been gaining valuable experience by playing abroad. And any of them have the flair to perform favourably in this tournament.

The 1994 World Cup finals produced much exciting and skilful football. But some countries competing in Euro 96 did not take part then: CROATIA, CZECH REPUBLIC, DENMARK, ENGLAND, FRANCE, PORTUGAL, SCOTLAND and TURKEY. And there have been several players who have matured into stars in the past two years: *Alessandro Del Piero* of ITALY, *Patrick Kluivert* and *Clarence Seedorf* of HOLLAND, *Heiko Herrlich* and *Christian Ziege* of GERMANY.

English club football was the most successful of all countries until the five-year ban imposed after the 1985 European Cup Final saw deaths at the Heysel Stadium in Brussels. Since then Manchester United and Arsenal have won editions of The Cup-Winners' Cup, and Arsenal was beaten by a goal in the 120th minute of the Cup-Winners' final in 1995. But there can be no doubt that it has suffered from becoming too insular, turning in on itself. Results in club competitions for the 1995/96 season were particularly disappointing.

But there have been increasing shafts of light from European players: *Eric Cantona* since 1991, and after the 1994 World Cup, the skill of *Jurgen Klinsmann*, *Brian Roy* and *Philippe Albert*. This has been reinforced in the past season by that of *Dennis Bergkamp* at Arsenal, *David Ginola* at Newcastle and *Ruud Gullit* at Chelsea.

We hope this book will also be useful when following other competitions. Much of the information given in EURO 96 could be of use for the final of the European club competitions in April and May 1996. And for the Olympic Games, which take place in August.

COUNT-DOWN TO THE FINAL

THE FOUR GROUPS

GROUP 'A'   Wembley in London (80,000)

Sat 8 June 3.00   England 1 v 1 Switzerland

Sat 15 June 3.00   England 2 v 0 Scotland

Tues 18 June 7.30   England 4 v 1 Holland

Villa Park in Birmingham (40,000)

Mon 10 June 4.30   Holland 0 v 0 Scotland

Thurs 13 June 7.30 Holland 2 v 0 Switzerland

Tues 18 June 7.30   Scotland 1 v 0 Switzerland

TEAM	P	W	D	L	F	A	Pts
1 England	3	2	1	0	7	2	7
2 Holland	3	1	1	1	3	4	4
3 Scotland	3	1	1	1	1	2	4
4 Switzerland	3	0	1	2	1	3	1

GROUP 'B'   Elland Road in Leeds (40,000)

Sun 9 June 2.30   Spain 1 v 1 Bulgaria

Sat 15 June 6.00   Spain 1 v 1 France

Tue 18 June 4.30   Spain 2 v 1 Rumania

St James's Park in Newcastle (40,000)

Mon 10 June 7.30	Rumania	0	v	1	France
Thur 13 June 4.30	Bulgaria	1	v	0	Rumania
Tues 18 June 4.30	Bulgaria	1	v	3	France

TEAM	P	W	D	L	F	A	Pts
1 France	3	2	1	0	5	2	7
2 Spain	3	1	2	0	4	3	5
3 Bulgaria	3	1	1	1	3	4	4
4 Romania	3	0	0	3	2	3	0

GROUP 'C'   Old Trafford in Manchester (55,000)

Sun 9 June 5.00	Germany	2	v	0	Czech Republic
Sun 16 June 3.00	Germany	3	v	0	Russia
Wed 19 June 7.30	Germany	0	v	0	Italy

Anfield in Liverpool (44,000)

Tues 11 June 4.30	Italy	2	v	1	Russia
Fri 14 June 7.30	Italy	1	v	2	Czech Republic
Wed 19 June 7.30	Russia	3	v	3	Czech Republic

TEAM	P	W	D	L	F	A	Pts
1 Germany	3	2	1	0	5	0	7
2 Czech Rep	3	1	1	1	5	6	4
3 Italy	3	1	1	1	3	3	4
4 Russia	3	0	1	2	4	8	1

GROUP 'D' Hillsborough in Sheffield (41,000)

Sun 9 June 7.30 .... Denmark **1** v **1** Portugal

Sun 16 June 6.00 .... Denmark **0** v **3** Croatia

Wed 19 June 4.30 .... Denmark **3** v **0** Turkey

The City Ground in Nottingham (35,000)

Tues 11 June 7.30 .... Croatia **1** v **0** Turkey

Fri 14 June 4.30 .... Portugal **1** v **0** Turkey

Wed 19 June 4.30 .... Portugal **3** v **0** Croatia

TEAM	P	W	D	L	F	A	Pts
1 Portugal	3	2	1	0	5	2	7
2 Croatia	3	2	0	1	4	3	6
3 Denmark	3	1	1	1	4	4	4
4 Turkey	3	0	0	3	0	5	0

QUARTER-FINALS

Sat 22 June **Wembley in London** 3.00

England **0** v **0** Spain
4-2 (peneltys)

Sat 22 June **Anfield in Liverpool** 6.30

France **0** v **0** Holland.
5-4 (peneltys)

Sun 23 June **Old Trafford in Manchester** 3.00

Germany **2** v **1** Croatia

Sun 23 June **Villa Park in Birmingham** 6.30

Portugal **0** v **1** Czech Rep.

SEMI-FINALS

Wed 26 June **Old Trafford in Manchester** 4.00

W Anfield ...... *France 0* ...... v W Villa Park *Czech Rep*
(4-5)

Wed 26 June **Wembley in London** 7.30

W Wembley ...... *England 0* ...... v W Old Trafford *1 Germany*
(5-6)

FINAL

Sun 30 June **Wembley in London** 7.00

...... *Czech Rep.* v *2 Germany* ......
(E.T)

The 8 cities in England where the 31 games will take place

❶ = London

❷ = Birmingham

❸ = Leeds

❹ = Newcastle

❺ = Manchester

❻ = Liverpool

❼ = Sheffield

❽ = Nottingham

SURPRISES IN THE QUALIFYING COMPETITION

As in 1992, the hosts were given automatic qualification, but not the holders, DENMARK. With three points now being given for a victory, there would be even more desire to win. A draw would be of little use. With the eight group leaders gaining automatic qualification, the games on the final day were vital in gaining that first place. So head-to-head confrontations gained more importance.

Group 1

FRANCE were unbeaten. But they made a slow start, before winning four of their last five matches and qualifying behind a *Hagi*-inspired RUMANIA.

Group 2

SPAIN were also unbeaten, a key result coming on 17 December 1994 when they travelled to Belgium and won 4-1. DENMARK also won in Belgium, and, by qualifying, compensated for being edged out of the 1994 World Cup by SPAIN.

Group 3

Much was expected of SWEDEN, who had finished third in both the previous tournament as well as the 1994 World Cup finals. But they threw away points. When SWITZERLAND (skilfully managed by *Roy Hodgson*) beat Turkey 2-1 in Istanbul, it was without their naturalised player, *Kubilay Turkilmaz*. He played for Galatasaray and feared for his fate if he should contribute in any manner to a Swiss success! TURKEY, however, won in Geneva, drew in Stockholm, and qualified behind SWITZERLAND. Euro 96 will be their first major championship since the 1954 World Cup.

Group 4

The first major upset came when ITALY, finalists in the World Cup, lost on 16 November 1994 in Palermo against CROATIA. CROATIA, entering their first competition, was blessed with some outstanding players including *Davor Suker*, the top scorer in the qualifying games. They went on to head the group, with ITALY finishing second.

Group 5

Another surprise took place when, on 7 June 1995, BELARUS beat HOLLAND, who fielded no less than seven players who'd helped Ajax win the European Cup two weeks earlier. This was emphasised in the return match, when HOLLAND did not get their only goal until the 84th minute. Top of the group was the CZECH REPUBLIC, who took 4 points off both HOLLAND and NORWAY, although the latter had long seemed destined to qualify. In the last game, however, when they needed just a draw, they lost 0-3 to HOLLAND.

Group 6

A polished PORTUGAL was always in convincing form, but the REPUBLIC OF IRELAND made life very hard-going for their manager, *Jack Charlton*, and their fans. A 1-0 victory against PORTUGAL in Dublin finished a run of five games which had brought 13 points. All the more disappointing, then, was the 0-0 draw away to LIECHTENSTEIN, despite having many opportunities to score, followed by two 3-1 defeats against AUSTRIA. A defence that had conceded only one goal in their previous six matches! Before the last match it seemed all set for AUSTRIA to qualify. It all depended on the final match. The REPUBLIC OF IRELAND lost 0-3 against PORTUGAL in Lisbon. But help was at hand 1000 miles to the north, in NORTHERN IRELAND, whose three losses had come in Belfast. In the end it was NORTHERN IRELAND's uplifting 5-3 win over a particularly uninspired AUSTRIA that helped their Irish cousins qualify for a play-off match against HOLLAND, the next team with the worst record in qualifying.

Group 7

BULGARIA made an emphatic start, winning their first six matches, only to lose out as group leaders to GERMANY, who won their last four. WALES, who might have provided a shock or two, were most disappointing. The best performance came in the 1-1 draw in Germany. But WALES did have two of the best 678 goals scored against them: *Balakov*'s fierce and curling drive in Sofia, and *Kinkladze*'s perfect 25-metre chip in Cardiff. GEORGIA had some most impressive results, including a 5-0 defeat of WALES, and a 2-1 defeat of BULGARIA.

Group 8

RUSSIA was undefeated: their only two draws came against the other side to qualify, SCOTLAND, who gave some gritty displays. Indeed, with Eastern Europe providing six of the finalists, RUSSIA could be a team to watch, depending on how well they blend together their foreign with their home talent.

Play-off

In the play-off match on 13 December 1995 at Anfield in Liverpool, HOLLAND beat the REPUBLIC OF IRELAND 2-0, and seemed to be finding the right blend to make them powerful in the summer. For IRELAND it brought back memories of 1966 when they were in another play-off, that time with SPAIN, at the Parc des Princes in Paris, only to lose 1-0.

The week following the play-off match, the REPUBLIC OF IRELAND's manager, *Jack Charlton*, offered his resignation to the Football Association of Ireland. It was duly accepted.

'Yes, I know who you are,' Pope John Paul remarked to an audience with *Charlton* and the 1990 World Cup team, 'You're the boss.' *Charlton* certainly was, and in the years after he became manager in January 1986 he took the REPUBLIC OF IRELAND to unknown territory. In the European championships he steered his team to qualifying in 1988, being beaten by ENGLAND on goal difference in 1992, and in 1996 to reaching the play-off stage. He also guided the team to take part in the final stages of the World Cup finals of 1990 and 1994.

Under his tutelage the record reads Played 93, Won 46, Drawn 30, Lost 17. *Mick McCarthy*, a former REPUBLIC OF IRELAND captain said of him, 'His secret is that the players trust him. He looks after his boys. He's very loyal.'

There were players that *Charlton* failed to use, and his direct style of tactics was sometimes criticised. He firmly believed that when his team has possession of the ball, it should make full use of it, never be vulnerable to counter-attacks, and 'must always be giving the opposition something to think about.' However, in the qualifying tournament, although 13 points came from the first five matches, the uplifting victory against PORTUGAL in Dublin was followed by a 0-0 draw in LIECHTENSTEIN and two 1-3 defeats against AUSTRIA. That single, lonely point from three matches during the summer had been crucial.

'We should have qualified by June,' remarked *Charlton* in resigned tones after IRELAND had been beaten in the play-off match. He was always likely to retire after the European Qualifying Championship, and anticipated IRELAND qualifying for the present tournament. Sadly, some key players were injured at crucial moments. But in his decade in charge *Jack Charlton* had become the man who 'has done for Ireland what none of us politicians could possibly achieve,' as admitted by Albert Reynolds, a former Irish Prime Minister.

Thanks to the 5-3 victory against AUSTRIA, NORTHERN IRELAND finished with an equal number of points to the REPUBLIC OF IRELAND. Had their home form not been so wretched, they could have been reaching the finals under *Bryan Hamilton*. And the sad record in the qualifying games from WALES, a country always capable of producing gifted players, could soon be forgotten with WALES having appointed a vibrant new manager in *Bobby Gould*.

The play-off match brought the qualifying rounds to a close. 47 countries had entered, and there had been 231 matches. FRANCE, RUSSIA and SPAIN had been unbeaten. There had been 680 goals, with RUSSIA having scored most (34), and FRANCE having conceded least (2).

THE COMPETING COUNTRIES

BULGARIA

GROUP B

Bulgarski Futbolen Soius founded in 1923. Joined FIFA 1924.

Previously qualified: Never.

Present tournament Finished second in Group 7 with 22 points from
10 games behind GERMANY (3-2 at home and 1-3 away)
but ahead of
GEORGIA (2-0 at home and 1-2 away)
MOLDOVA (4-1 at home and 3-0 away)
WALES (3-0 away and 3-1 at home)
ALBANIA (1-1 away and 3-0 at home)

The manager *Dimitar Penev* (50) spent thirteen seasons as a player with
CSKA Sofia, and gained 90 caps as a central defender, followed by five
years of successful coaching with CSKA. It is a compact squad, and many of
his star players perform in high-pressure leagues outside BULGARIA. One
of the highlights of the 1994 World Cup finals, when Bulgaria reached the
semi-final stage, was the victory over the holders, GERMANY, at the
quarter-final stage. The subsequent confidence was shown by BULGARIA
winning the first six matches in the qualifying tournament; in one of them
they again defeated GERMANY.

The goalkeepers will be the experienced *Borislav Mikhailov* (34) with
Dimitar Popov (26) as his deputy.

The defence in front is solid with *Petar Khubchev* (32), a most effective sweeper, with *Valentin Dartilov* (29) as his deputy. In front are *Emil Kremenliev* (26), *Trifon Ivanov* (30), *Ilian Kiriakov* (28), and on the left is *Zanko Zvetanov* (26), who joined Waldhof Mannheim in 1995.

The midfield has been outstanding with the goal-scoring *Nasko Sirakov* (34 on 26 April), and *Yordan Letchkov* (28), one of the stars of the 1994 World Cup. In 1995 three players joined teams in the demanding German Bundesliga - the creative *Krasimir Balakov* (30), who joined VfB Dortmund, the defensive *Zlatko Yankov* (29) who joined Bayer Uerdingen, and *Daniel Borimov* (26) who joined 1860 Munich.

In the attack have been the much-travelled *Emil Kostadinov* (28), at present with Bayern Munich, and the prolific *Hristo Stoichkov* (30), now with Parma. Support comes from Dimitar's nephew *Liuboslov Penev* (29), now with Atletico Madrid.

The top scorer was *Stoichkov* with 9 of the 22 goals; *Kostadinov* scored 7.

CROATIA

GROUP D

Croatia Football Federation founded 1991. Joined FIFA 1991.

Previously qualified: Never.

Present tournament Headed Group 3 with 23 points from 10 games
against ITALY (2-1 away and 1-1 at home)
LITHUANIA (2-0 at home and 0-0 away)
UKRAINE (4-0 at home and 0-1 away)
SLOVENIA (2-0 at home and 2-1 away)
ESTONIA (7-1 at home and 2-0 away)

The manager who guided CROATIA through the qualifying round was
Miroslav Blazevic (55). Having managed club sides in France, Greece and
Switzerland, he was ideal to replace the respected *Tomislav Ivic*.

The goalkeeper has been *Drazen Ladic* (33) with his deputies *Tonci
Gabric* (35), and *Marijan Mrmic* (31 on 6 May).

The defence has three central defenders in *Nikola Jerkan* (31) of Real
Oviedo, who plays as sweeper; *Igor Stimac* (28), who in October 1995
moved from Hajduk Split to Derby County; or *Dzevad Turkovic* (24 on 17
June), and *Slaven Bilic* (27). There will be two lateral full-backs, *Nikola
Jurkevic* (29) on the right, and on the left the attacking-minded *Robert Jarni*
(27) who has just moved from Juventus to Real Betis.

In midfield may be the highly talented *Zvonimir Boban* (27), who has
been appearing in Italy for Bari and A.C. Milan; *Robert Prosinecki* (27), who
has just joined Barcelona; the experienced *Alijosa Asamovic* (30), now with
Real Valladolid; the defensive *Zoran Stanic* (28), or *Mladen Mladenovic* (31).

Up front will be two strikers - *Alen Boksic* (26) who has been making and scoring goals for Lazio after spells with Hajduk Split and Marseille, whom he helped to win the 1993 European Cup; and the deadly *Davor Suker* (28) of Seville. The reserves have been *Ardian Kozniku* (28) with Cannes, *Ivica Mornar* (22) and *Goran Vlaovic* (23) with Padova.

The top scorer was *Suker* with 12 of the 22 goals.

The disintegration of the former Yugoslavia has meant the creation of several smaller states, none more formidable than Croatia. Many Croatian players star in Belgium, Germany, Holland, Italy and Spain.

'Croatia will be the revelation of this qualification tournament,' *Blazevic* has claimed. 'There is a fine team. It just needs playing together.'

REPRESENTATION OF CZECHS AND SLOVAKS

GROUP C

Ceskolovensky Fotbalovy Svaz founded in 1881. Joined FIFA 1906.

Previously qualified: 1960 (3rd), 1976 (1st) and 1980 (3rd).

Present tournament First in Group 5 with 21 points from 10 games ahead of
HOLLAND (0-0 away and 3-1 at home)
NORWAY (1-1 away and 2-0 at home)
BELARUS (4-2 at home and 2-0 away)
LUXEMBOURG (0-1 away and 3-0 at home)
MALTA (6-1 at home and 0-0 away)

The manager *Dusan Uhrin* (52) took over after a most successful thirty-month spell as coach to Sparta Prague, whom he led to great success in the 1992/93 European Cup, and then the 1993/94 Cup-Winners' Cup.

The goalkeepers have been the outstanding *Petr Kouba* (26) of Sparta Prague and *Pavel Srnicek* (28) of Newcastle United, but *Ludek Miklosko* (34) of West Ham United might be considered.

The defence has seen *Jan Suchoparek* (26), a commanding sweeper who starred in the 1992 Olympic Games, and Sparta Prague's *Jiri Novotny* (26 on 7 April) as stopper. Others who have played have been *Tomas Repka* (22) of Sparta Prague; and the experienced *Miroslav Kadlec* (32 on 22 June) of Kaiserslautern who played in the 1990 World Cup finals; Schalke's *Radoslav Latal* (26), who sometimes plays in midfield; and *Martin Kotulek* (26).

The midfield has Sparta Prague's *Martyn Frydeck* (27), who scored the opening goal in Minsk against Belorussia; the promising *Patrik Berger* (22) of Borussia Dortmund, the German champions; *Vaclav Nemecek* (29); the left-footed *Lubos Kubik* (32) now playing in Germany; *Jiri Nemec* (30 on 15 May), a fast-moving right-sided midfielder; *Daniel Smejkal* (25), who is superb with free kicks, and *Pavel Nedved* (23) of Sparta Prague.

The forwards will be drawn from *Pavel Kuka* (27), who plays in Germany for Kaiserslautern, the prolific *Horst Siegl* (27), and the tall and imposing *Tomas Skhuravy* (31). But others who might feature are *Vratislav Lokvenc* (22) and *Jan Koller* (23) - the tall pair of promising young strikers from Sparta Prague - and *Radek Drulak* (34).

The top scorer with 5 of the 21 goals was *Berger*.

CZECKOSLOVAKIA's last match was the 0-0 draw with BELGIUM in November 1993, when a win could have seen them playing in the 1994 World Cup. The first game of the CZECH REPUBLIC was the 4-1 win in February 1994 in Istanbul against TURKEY.

It was a varied qualifying tournament. The loss to LUXEMBOURG was most humiliating, but the wins against HOLLAND and NORWAY have been uplifting.

DENMARK

SEEDED GROUP D

Federation Dansk Boldspil-Union founded 1889. Joined FIFA 1904.

Previously qualified: 1964 (4th), 1984 (Semi-finalist), 1988, 1992 (1st).

Present tournament Second in Group 2 with 21 points from 10
games behind SPAIN (0-3 away and 1-1 at home)
but ahead of
BELGIUM (3-1 at home and 3-1 away)
MACEDONIA (1-1 away and 1- 0 at home)
CYPRUS (1-1 away and 4-0 at home)
ARMENIA (2-0 away and 3-1 at home)

The manager *Richard Moller-Nielsen* (58) had his playing career cut
short by injury, turned to coaching, and in thirteen years with OB Odense,
won the League twice. He came into charge of DENMARK in the spring of
1990, and saw a fairy-tale ending to the 1992 European Nations
Championship: DENMARK, at the last moment, replaced the banished
YUGOSLAVIA (due to the civil war), and won! Although beaten in their
last qualifying match for the 1994 World Cup by a single, controversial goal
by SPAIN (*Hierro* heading home after *Schmeichel* had been deliberately
blocked), they entered and won the Intercontinental Cup final 2-0 against
ARGENTINA in January 1995 in Saudi Arabia.

The goalkeepers have been *Peter Schmeichel* (32) of Manchester United
with *Mogens Kroch* (32) of Brondby as his deputy.

The defence will have *Thomas Helveg* (25 on 6 June) from Udinese;
Jacob Laursen (26); the imposing *Marc Rieper* (28 on 20 June) of West
Ham; *Jes Hogh* (30 on 7 May); the long-lasting *Lars Olsen* (35); *Jens Risager*

(25 on 9 April) of Brondby; *Jacob Kjeldbjerg* (26) of Chelsea; *Torben Piechnik* (33 on 21 May); and *Jakob Friis-Hansen* (33 on 21 May).

In midfield will be the opportunist *Kim Vilfort* (33), who scored crucial goals against BELGIUM and SPAIN; the celebrated *Michael Laudrup* (32 on 15 June), who now plays for Real Madrid; and *John Jensen* (31 on 3 May) of Arsenal. Others include *Henrik Jensen* (36); *Brian Steen Nielsen* (27); *Henrik Larsen* (30 on 17 May); and *Allan Nielsen* (25) of Brondby, who scored the crucial second goal in the away-tie against ARMENIA on his debut, only 30 seconds after coming on as a substitute.

In the attack will be *Brian Laudrup* (27), now with Glasgow Rangers; but his former partner *Fleming Poulsen* (29) of Borussia Dortmund suffered an injury in 1994. *Bent Christensen* (29), who in 1995 joined Compostela from Olympiakos, is available. And two forwards who have recently been chosen are *Mikkel Beck* (23 on 12 May), and *Peter Rasmussen* (29 on 16 May) of AaB Aalborg, who has experience of playing with VfB Stuttgart.

The top scorer with 5 of the 19 goals was *Vilfort*.

ENGLAND

SEEDED GROUP A

Football Association founded 1863. Joined FIFA 1905-1920, 1924-28, 1946.

Previously qualified: 1968 (3rd), 1980, 1988 and 1992.

Present tournament Qualified automatically as hosts.

The manager *Terry Venables* (53) knew success as a coach with Crystal Palace, Queens Park Rangers, Barcelona in Spain (where he was voted Manager of the Year for 1985), and Tottenham Hotspur. He became manager in March 1994 after ENGLAND's unsuccessful bid to qualify for the 1994 World Cup finals. He has played as many games as possible, with the first defeat not coming until the 3-1 loss to BRAZIL in June 1995. Most of these have been 'friendlies' which have lacked the cutting edge of games inside a competition, but have been used to judge the most appropriate strengths for each occasion.

The goalkeepers will be *David Seaman* (32), who has experienced much success with Arsenal, and *Tim Flowers* (29) with Blackburn Rovers.

In the defence have been, at right-back *Rob Jones* (24) of Liverpool, the much-improved *Gary Neville* (21) of Manchester United; and at left-back Blackburn's *Graeme Le Saux* (27) or *Stuart Pearce* (34 on 24 April) of Nottingham Forest, who played in the 1990 World Cup and the 1992 European Championship. In the centre of the defence have been players with much-valued experience with their clubs - Arsenal's long-serving stopper *Tony Adams* (29), who played in the 1988 tournament, and *Gary Pallister* (31 on 30 June) of Manchester United. The impressive *Colin Cooper* (29) of Nottingham Forest, and the mobile *Steve Howey* (24) of Newcastle United are others who have been selected.

Inspiring the midfield has been *Paul Gascoigne* (29 on 23 May) who has recovered superbly from two serious leg injuries; alongside him is the goal-scoring *David Platt* (30 on 10 June). In the holding role in midfield have been Newcastle's *Robert Lee* (30), who has had a splendid season, *Paul Ince* (29), formerly with Manchester United and now with Internazionale, and *David Batty* (28) of Blackburn Rovers. But the fluent *Gareth Southgate* (25) made a most impressive debut against Portugal in December. The revitalized *John Barnes* (32), who was first selected in 1983, and *Dennis Wise* (29) of Chelsea have been midfield prompters. But younger players of potential have included the much-improved *Jamie Redknapp* (23 on 25 June). Others are the free-running *Nick Barmby* (22), who in 1995 left Tottenham Hotspur for Middlesborough; Liverpool's exciting *Steve McManaman* (24); and the lissom, left-sided *Darren Anderton* (24) who will play wide and offer options. *Steve Stone* (24) of Nottingham Forest played an excellent game against SWITZERLAND in November 1994, making one goal and scoring another; and the lively *Trevor Sinclair* (23) is another player of rare talent.

In the attack have been *Alan Shearer* (25), who's been on prolific form for Blackburn, and *Teddy Sheringham* (30) who has the rare gift of creating as well as scoring goals for his team, Tottenham Hotspur. In addition have been *Les Ferdinand* (29) and the creative *Peter Beardsley* (35), his colleague at Newcastle United, who played in the World Cups of 1986 and 1990, and the 1988 European Championship. But *Andy Cole* (24), now with Manchester United, will be trying to revive the lethal form he showed with Newcastle United. The Liverpool pair of the promising *Robbie Fowler* (21) and *Stan Collymore* (25) might also be used.

FRANCE

GROUP B

Federation Francaise de Football founded 1919. Joined FIFA 1919.

Previously qualified: 1960, 1984 (1st), 1992.

Present tournament Second in Group 1 with 20 points from 10
games behind RUMANIA (0-0 at home and 3-1 away)
but ahead of
POLAND (1-1 at home and 0-0 away)
ISRAEL (0-0 away and 2-0 at home)
SLOVAKIA (0-0 away and 4-0 at home)
AZERBAIDJAN (2-0 away and 10-0 at home)

The manager The former coach to Bordeaux and Montpellier *Aimé
Jacquet* (56) was appointed after the failure to qualify for the 1994 finals.
That was an unforeseen humiliation for FRANCE, since only one point was
required from the final two home matches against ISRAEL and
BULGARIA. Both were lost, even though FRANCE scored first, with the
deciding final goals coming in the 90th minute! There was an icy degree of
shock, followed by an inevitable hangover. FRANCE made extremely hard
going of qualifying on this occasion, unlike in 1992, when they qualified
with a 100 per cent record. There were four 0-0 draws in the first five games,
and they drew the seventh game 1-1 after failing to convert a penalty. All
came right, however, with the record-breaking 10-0 win against
AZERBAIDJAN, the crucial 3-1 victory against RUMANIA in Bucharest,
and the 2-0 victory against ISRAEL.

The goalkeepers In nine of the games the goalkeeper has been *Bernard
Lama* (33 on 17 April) with Paris Saint Germain. His reserve has been
Fabian Barthez (24) of Monaco; *Bruno Martini* (34), who played in the 1992
finals, is in good form.

The defence At right-back will be the Turin-based *Jocelyn Angloma* (30)
- the only one who played in all ten matches, or *Lilian Thuram* (24) of
Monaco; and on the left *Eric Di Meco* (32) or *Bixente Lizarazu* (26).
Auxerre's *Laurent Blanc* (30) is a very assured sweeper who likes to attack.
In the vital 3-1 win in Rumania *Frank Leboeuf* (28) played superbly. Paris
Saint Germain's *Alain Roche* (28) is a stopper who marks tightly.

The midfield is bursting with talent. The Milan-based *Marcel Desailly*
(27) is a sweeper in front of the defence with, on his right, *Didier
Deschamps* (27) of Juventus, and, on his left, *Vincent Guerin* (30). Others
include *Paul Le Guen* (32), a skilled midfielder with the hardest shot in
French football, the exciting *Christian Karembeu* (25), who joined
Sampdoria in 1995, and the left-sided *Zinedine Zidane* (23). *Reynald Pedros*
(24), a speedy winger, has scored some thunderous goals for his club,
Nantes; *Youri Djorkaeff* (27), who in 1995 moved from Monaco to Paris SG,
has been on incisive form; *Patrick Vieira* (20), who transferred from Cannes
to A.C. Milan, might be called in at the last minute.

The attack has *Patrick Loko* (26) from Paris SG; *Nicolas Ouedec* (24)
from the French 1995 champions Nantes; alongside him is *Christophe
Dugarry* (24) of Bordeaux. But playing outside are the highly-talented *David
Ginola* (29), and, given that *Jean-Pierre Papin* (32) has been little used by
Bayern Munich, France might still have need of the genius of *Eric Cantona*
(30 on May 25).

The leading scorer with 5 of the 22 goals was *Djorkaeff*.

GERMANY

SEEDED GROUP C

Deutscher Fussball-Bund founded in 1900. Joined FIFA in 1904-1945, 1950.

Previously qualified: 1972 (1st), 1976 (2nd), 1980 (1st), 1984, 1988 (semi-finalist) and 1992 (2nd).

Present tournament First in Group 7 with 25 points from 10 games ahead of
BULGARIA (2-3 away and 3-1 at home)
GEORGIA (2- 0 away and 4-1 at home)
MOLDOVA (3-0 away and 6-1 at home)
ALBANIA (3-0 away and 6-1 at home)
WALES (1-1 at home and 2-1 away)

The manager *'Berti'* Vogts (49) was right-back during the 1970s when WEST GERMANY won the 1972 European Championship and the 1974 World Cup. He also knew many triumphs with Borussia Moenchengladbach. After eleven years as coach with the DFB, he took over after the victory in the 1990 finals and steered GERMANY to become beaten finalists in the 1992 European Championship. In this campaign it squandered a 2-0 lead against BULGARIA in Sofia to concede three goals between the 44th and 69th minutes. That, however, was the only defeat, and in the final match against BULGARIA, GERMANY was most impressive.

The goalkeepers have normally been *Andreas Kopke* (34) with *Oliver Kahn* (27 on 15 June) from Bayern Munich as his deputy.

In defence the highly experienced *Lothar Matthaus* (35) has been replaced as sweeper. *Matthias Sammer* (28) is a strong-running forager playing behind *Stefan Reuter* (29) or the poised *Thomas Helmer* (31 on 21 April); the tall, authoritative *Jurgen Kohler* (30) has returned after five seasons with Juventus in Italy. At right back could be *Markus Babbel* (23) of Bayern Munich; at left-back could be the exciting *Christian Ziege* (24).

In the midfield will be the gifted *Andreas Moeller* (28), who has been on outstanding form, as has *Thomas Haessler* (30 on 30 May), and *Thomas Strunz* (28 on 25 April). But the attack-minded *Mario Basler* (27) and *Dieter Eilts* (31) of Werder Bremen have been brought in, as has *Steffen Freund* (26) of Borussia Dortmund.

In the attack will be the gifted *Jurgen Klinsmann* (31) who plays for Bayern Munich after his splendid season with Tottenham. *Karlheinz Riedle* (30) came back successfully from a serious injury. But others who have also played have been the newcomer *Heiko Herrlich* (24) who in 1995 left Borussia Moenchengladbach for Borussia Dortmund, and *Ulf Kirsten* (30).

The chief scorer with 9 of the 27 goals was *Klinsmann*.

Berti Vogts seems to have blended a strong cocktail of experience (*Helmer*, *Kohler*, *Hassler*, *Moller*, *Riedle*, *Klinsmann*) mixed with new players (*Babbel*, *Freund*, *Ziege*, *Basler*, *Herrlich*). As so often, Germany will be among the teams to beat.

HOLLAND

GROUP A

Dutch Football League founded in 1889. Joined FIFA 1924.

Previously qualified: 1976 (3rd), 1980, 1988 (1st) and 1992 (semi-finalist).

Present competition Finished second in Group 5 with 20 points from 10 games behind CZECH REPUBLIC (0-0 at home and 1-3 away) but ahead of
NORWAY (1-1 away and 3-0 at home)
LUXEMBOURG (4-0 away and 5-0 at home)
BELARUS 0-1 away and 1-0 at home)
MALTA (4-0 at home and 4-0 away)

Won the match against IRELAND in the play-off eliminator in December 1995.

The manager HOLLAND were guided through the first three games by *Dick Advocaat* who had taken them to the quarter-finals of the 1994 World Cup. After his resignation, the man put in charge wasthe ex PSV Eindhoven and Valencia coach, *Guus Hiddink* (47). Unlike the Irish, HOLLAND started hesitantly, and took only 11 points from the first seven games. But 9 points came from the last three, when HOLLAND built their team around Ajax players, past and present. In the play-off match, they used ten of these.

The goalkeepers will be *Edwin Van Der Sar* (26) of Ajax Amsterdam, with *Ed De Goey* (29) of Feyenoord as his deputy.

The defence can call upon *Michael Reiziger* (23); the experienced *Danny Blind* (34); *Frank De Boer* (26 on 15 May). They have all been on outstanding form with Ajax Amsterdam. Their club colleague *Winston Bogarde* (25) played impressively in the play-off match; and *Stan Valckx*

(32) of PSV Eindhoven, *Orlando Trustfull* (25) of Feyenoord and
Arthur Numan (26) from PSV Eindhoven are others who have played.

In midfield could be the experienced *Rob Witschge* (29) of Feyenoord and
two new stars: the defensive *Clarence Seedorf* (20 on 1 April), who in 1995
joined Sampdoria from Ajax just after they'd won the European Cup, and
Edgar Davids (23) of Ajax Amsterdam. The hard-working *Wim Jonk* (29)
has returned to Holland after two years with Inter in Italy and now plays
for PSV Eindhoven; others might be *Ronald De Boer* (26 on 15 May) and
the Rome-based attacking midfielder *Aron Winter* (26).

The attack could be represented by *Dennis Bergkamp* (27) who is back
scoring goals with Arsenal after his two barren years with Inter; *Youri
Mulder* (27) of Schalke '04, who scored the only goal in the 84th minute
against Belarus. Great things are promised by *Patrick Kluivert* (19) of Ajax.
Among those providing service could be *Marc Overmars* (23), an outside-
left of great potential who scores crucial goals; *Glenn Helder* (27) of
Arsenal; and the highly-talented *Brian Roy* (26), now with Nottingham
Forest.

The top scorers with 4 of the 25 goals was *Overmars*.

Gone are the days of 'Total Football', and the stars of the victorious 1988
team have all retired from the international game. But as the club sides of
Ajax, Feyenoord and PSV Eindhoven show, Dutch football always produces
a thrilling mixture of great skill and tactical sophistication. Although, as so
often, they struggled to qualify, HOLLAND could be ranked with the sides
of 1988, when they won, and 1992, when they played some of the best
football.

ITALY

GROUP C

Federazione Italiana Giuoco Calcio founded 1898. Joined FIFA 1905.

Previously qualified: 1968 (1st), 1980 (4th) and 1988 (Semi-finalist).

Present tournament Finished second in Group 4 with 23 points from
10 games behind CROATIA (1-2 at home and 1-1 away)
but in front of
LITHUANIA (1-0 away and 4-0 at home)
UKRAINE (2-0 away and 4-1 at home)
SLOVENIA (1-1 away and 1-0 at home)
ESTONIA (2-0 away and 4-1 at home)

The manager has been *Arrigo Sacchi* (40 on 1 April) who coached
Parma and gained many honours with A.C. Milan after he moved to them
in 1987. He took over as manager of ITALY after the failure to qualify for
the 1992 European Championship; his first match was in November 1991.
Blessed with a stroke or three of luck and superb goals from *Roberto Baggio*,
ITALY eventually finished as finalists in the 1994 World Cup tournament.

The goalkeeper has varied. The experienced *Gianluca Pagliuca* (29) of
Internazionale has recently lost form, but *Angelo Peruzzi* (26) of Juventus
has been imposing, and the youthful *Francesco Toldo* (24) of Fiorentina has
been most impressive.

The defence will be drawn from *Ciro Ferrara* (29), who might play as
libero, alongside *Alessandro Costacurta* (30 on 24 April) as stopper, or *Luigi
Apolloni* (29 on 2 May). *Antonio Benarrivo* (27) could be right-back, with
the outstanding *Paolo Maldini* (28 on 26 June) as left-back. The reserves
will be *Moreno Torricelli* (26), and *Amedeo Carboni* (31 on 6 May).

In midfield will be *Dino Baggio* (24), now with Parma; the authoritative *Demetrio Albertini* (24); *Roberto Di Matteo* (26 on 29 May), who has been on good form for Lazio; *Angelo Di Livio* (29); and also from Juventus the outstanding *Alessandro Del Piero* (21). Others might include *Massimo Crippa* (31 on 17 May) of Parma, *Francesco Statuto* (24) and *Antonio Conte* (26) of Juventus.

The attack could feature the sublime artistry of that astute goal-scorer *Roberto Baggio* (29). But the industrious *Fabrizio Ravanelli* (27) of Juventus and Parma's *Gianfranco Zola* (30 on 5 July) have been chosen recently. Others Sacchi might choose include the pacy *Giuseppe Signori* (28), *Pierluigi Casiraghi* (27), who both play for Lazio, or *Marco Simone* (27) of A.C. Milan.

The top scorer with 6 of the 20 goals was *Zola*.

Four points from the first three games, then four victories: Italy frequently makes extremely enigmatic work of qualifying.

However, given the professionalism, flair and success of their club game, Italy will certainly be a team to look out for.

PORTUGAL

GROUP D

Federacio Federcalcao Portuguesa de Futebol founded 1914. Joined FIFA 1926.

Previously qualified: 1984 (Semi-finalist).

Present tournament Finished top of Group 6 with 23 points from 10 games against
REPUBLIC OF IRELAND (0-1 away and 3-0 at home)
AUSTRIA (1-0 at home and 1-1 away)
NORTHERN IRELAND (2-1 away and 1-1 at home)
LATVIA (3-1 away and 3-2 at home)
LIECHTENSTEIN (8-0 at home and 7-0 away)

The manager who guided Portugal to their first participation in a major championship since 1966 was *Antonio Luis Oliviera* (46). He started his career as a coach at only 29 with the local side of Penafiel, before moving on to play for and coach Sporting Lisbon. He took over in June 1994, and has been blessed with working with players of rare talent, who have been together in successful youth squads of 1989 and 1991 (*Couto, Figo, Joao Pinto, Rui Costa*).

Portugal will relish bringing back memories of 1966. This time they will play with great flair, but perhaps they lack a good marksman such as *Eusebio* who became top scorer 30 years ago.

The goalkeeper is the much-praised *Vitor Baia* (26) from the 1995 champions FC Porto, managed by Bobby Robson, with his deputy *Neno* (34) of Vitoria.

The defence has *Fernando Couto* (26) as sweeper, who in 1994 left Porto to join Parma in Italy. He plays behind the big *Helder* (25) of Benfica, who scored against IRELAND in Lisbon. Others chosen are *Paulo Madeira* (25) and *Jorge Costa* (24) from Porto. *Joao Domingos Pinto* (34), who played in the 1986 World Cup, played in several matches. Both 'wing-backs', *Carlos Secretario* (26 on May 12) and *Paulinho Santos* (25), who scored the goal in Vienna, are from Porto. Benfica's *Dimas* (27) is also a skilful left-sided defender.

In midfield will be the strong *Oceano* (33) from Sporting, who plays as a barrier in front of the defence. The others include the talented *Paolo Souza* (25), who left Sporting to join Juventus in 1994; *Vitor Paneira* (30); and the goal-scoring *Rui Costa* (24), who left Benfica to join Fiorentina in 1994. The exciting *Luis Figo* (23), coveted by both Juventus and Parma, instead joined Barcelona in 1995. *Rui Barros* (30), who is with FC Porto but has experience of playing with Juventus, could be the link between midfield and the attack.

In the attack could be the magical and much-travelled (Atletico Madrid, Olympique Marseille, Reggiana) *Paulo Futre* (30), now with A.C. Milan, who played in the 1986 World Cup, and the outstanding *Joao Viera Pinto* (24). *Sa Pinto* (23) played in some early games, but *Domingos Oliviera* (26) and *Antonio Folha* (25 on 21 May) from Porto and *Jorge Cadette* (27), who scored against IRELAND, have been in form.

The leading scorer with 6 goals of the 29 goals was *Domingos*.

RUMANIA

GROUP B

Federatia Romana de Fotbal founded in 1908. Joined FIFA 1929.

Previously qualified: 1984.

Present tournament Finished top of Group 1 with 21 points from 10 games against
FRANCE (0-0 away and 1-3 at home)
POLAND (2-1 at home and 0-0 away)
ISRAEL (1-1 away and 2-1 at home)
SLOVAKIA (3-2 at home and 2-0 away)
AZERBAJAN (3-0 at home and 4-1 away)

The manager *Anghel Iordanescu* (46 on May 4) took over after the 5-2 defeat by the REPRESENTATION OF THE CZECHS AND SLOVAKS in June 1993. RUMANIA eventually qualified for the 1994 World Cup finals by defeating WALES 2-1 in Cardiff. It played some fine counter-attacking football during the tournament, losing at the quarter-final stage to SWEDEN. But the team has remained together, and qualification for the present tournament was almost guaranteed by gaining 17 points from their first seven matches.

The goalkeepers are *Bogdan Stelea* (28), who is with Steaua Bucharest after spells in Spain, Belgium and Turkey, and *Florian Prunea* (27).

The defence *Dan Petrescu* (28), who joined Chelsea from Sheffield Wednesday in late 1995, is an attacking right-back, and *Daniel Prodan* (24) of Steaua Bucharest is at left-back. In the centre of the defence *Gheorghe Mihali* (30), now with Guincamp in France, and *Tibor Selymes* (26 on 14 May) have played. Behind them has been a *libero* of great poise in *Miodrag Belodedic* (32 on 20 May), with *Anton Dobos* (30) of Steaua Bucharest as his deputy.

The key player in midfield is the mercurial *Gheorghe Hagi* (31).
Alongside him are *Ioan Sabau* (28); the experienced *Gheorghe Popescu* (28);
the goal-scoring *Ilie Dumitrescu* (26), who has rejoined Tottenham Hotspur
after his loan spell to Seville; *Ionut Lupescu* (27); and *Daniel Munteanu* (28
on 25 June). The experienced *Marius Lacatus* (32 on 5 April) has returned
to Steaua Bucharest after spells in Italy and Spain and drops back as a wide
midfielder.

The star of the attack will be Espanol's *Florian Raduciou* (26 on 17
March). Alongside him will be *Ion Vladiou* (27) and *Adrian Ilie* (29 on 20
April), who has been on lethal form for Steaua Bucharest.

The leading scorer with 5 of the 18 goals was *Raduciou.*

Iordanescu will be hoping that his experienced side starts to show the
impetus they did two years ago, when they played thrilling games against
ARGENTINA and SWEDEN. He will hope, above all, that RUMANIA
don't have to leave the competition after a penalty shoot-out: this has been
their lot in the last two World Cups!

RUSSIA

GROUP C

Russian Football Union founded 1991. Joined FIFA 1991.

Previously qualified: As USSR 1960 (1st), 1964 (2nd), 1968 (4th), 1972 (2nd), 1988 (2nd), and as CIS 1992.

The present tournament Finished first in Group 8 with 26 points from 10 games ahead of
SCOTLAND (1-1 away and 0-0 at home)
GREECE (2-1 at home and 3-0 away)
FINLAND (6-0 away and 3-1 at home)
FAROE ISLANDS (3-0 at home and 5-2 away)
SAN MARINO (4-0 at home and 7-0 away)

The manager The fragmentation of the Soviet Union in December 1991 into various states has meant a weakening of the national team. In the past they had relied on stars from the Ukraine in particular. In fact the team that played in the 1992 European Championship was the last drawn from all the states, and eventually RUSSIA was declared as the inheritor of the Soviet Union's membership. But no less than seven leading players (*Shalimov*, the alleged ringleader, *Kolyvanov, Kiriakov, Kanchelskis, Kulkov, Dobrovolski* and *Ivanov*) refused to participate in the 1994 World Cup; and, after it, the manager *Pavel Saydrin* was replaced by *Oleg Romantsev* (52), who also manages Moscow Spartak. In the circumstances it is no surprise that in the home game against the FAROE ISLANDS he used ten of their players! His main task has been to unite the home-based players with the foreign mercenaries. And although critics thought he couldn't perform both tasks, both his teams have triumphed superbly.

The goalkeepers have been *Dmitri Kharin* (27) of Chelsea and his rival *Stanislav Cherchesov* (32), who is with Spartak Moscow.

The defence has the outstanding *Yuri Nikiforov* (25) playing as sweeper behind the regular choices as stoppers in the Spartak Moscow defence: *Andrei Ivanov* (29 on 6 April) and the powerful *Victor Onopko* (26), who is the perfect link between midfield and defence. *Ramiz Mamedow* (24) has also played. *Dmitri Khlestov* (25) is at right-back and at left-back *Ilia Tsimbalar* (27 on 17 June), who played in 1994, or *Yuri Kovtun* (26).

The midfield will be organised by *Valeri Karpin* (27) of Estonia. From Spartak Moscow, the left-footed *Andrei Piatnitski* (29) and influential *Vasili Kulkov* (30 on 11 June) are also available. Others who have played include *Igor Dobrovolski* (28) from Moldavia; *Igor Shalimov* (27); playing wide, *Andrei Kanchelskis* (27), now with Everton; and *Aleksandr Mostovoi* (27), who did play in 1994, despite initially not wishing to.

In the attack will be *Sergei Yuran* (27 on 11 June). Like *Cherchesov* and *Kulkov*, he has rejoined Moscow Spartak. Alongside him could be *Sergei Kiriakov* (26), *Dmitri Radchenko* (26), and *Igor Kolyvanov* (26). *Oleg Salenko* (26) of Glasgow Rangers, who scored a record five goals in a match during the 1994 World Cup, was never used. RUSSIA still scored the largest number of goals of any country in qualifying.

The leading scorer with 5 of the 34 goals was *Kolyvanov*.

SCOTLAND

GROUP A

Scottish Football Association founded in 1873. Joined FIFA 1910-20, 1924-28, 1946.

Previously qualified: 1992.

Present tournament Second in Group 8 with 23 points from 10 games behind RUSSIA (1-1 at home and 0-0 away)
but ahead of
GREECE (0-1 away and 1-0 at home)
FINLAND (2-0 away and 1-0 at home)
FAROES (5-1 at home and 2-0 away)
SAN MARINO (2- 0 away and 5-0 at home)

The manager The much-respected former coach *Craig Brown* (55) succeeded *Andy Roxborough* who had taken the team to the finals of both the 1990 World Cup and the 1992 European Championships. Gaining two draws with RUSSIA was a considerable achievement, but the self-effacing *Brown* remarked that if 'we get five wins from our next five matches, we should be all right.' They did, and were.

The goalkeepers have been *Andy Goram* (32 on 13 April), who has been on outstanding form for Rangers, and *Jim Leighton* (37) of Hibernian. He played some outstanding games when *Goram* was injured, particularly in Moscow against RUSSIA, when he made some breathtaking saves.

The defence will be drawn from, at right-back *Stewart McKimmie* (33) of Aberdeen; Celtic's *Tommy Boyd* (30) has been in grand form, as has his clubmate *Tosh McKinlay* (31), who gave an accomplished debut in the home match against GREECE. The resolute *Colin Hendry* (30) from Blackburn Rovers has been an excellent stopper; alongside him *Alan*

McLaren (25), who has been gaining experience with Rangers; and the much-chosen *Craig Levein* (31) of Hearts. *Colin Calderwood* (30) of Tottenham Hotspur made his debut in Moscow in March 1995 when *Brown* successfully chose three centre-backs.

There is a very strong midfield with the ball-winning *Stuart McCall* (32 on 10 June) of Rangers and the influential *Gary McAllister* (31) of Leeds United who both played in 1992. The experienced *Paul McStay* (31) appeared, as did his club partner at Celtic *John Collins* (27), who played some outstanding games and is powerful in the opposition area. Others to appear were *Craig Burley* (24) of Chelsea; *Billy McKinlay* (27), who in October 1995 moved from Dundee United to Blackburn Rovers; and *Scott Gemmill* (25) of Nottingham Forest, who was chosen very late.

Up front, the evergreen *Ally McCoist* (33) of Rangers has made a great comeback from injury in 1993, and his great experience could be crucial. The tall *Duncan Ferguson* (24) of Everton can be most threatening, if he recovers form after being imprisoned for head-butting an opponent. The incisive in-form *Scott Booth* (24) scored in the last four games. *Eion Jess* (25), his partner at Aberdeen, and the experienced *Pat Nevin* (31), who played in the 1992 tournament, have provided an excellent service. The former Rangers player *John Spencer* (25), now with Chelsea, also might be chosen.

The leading scorer with 5 of the 19 goals was *Collins*.

SPAIN

SEEDED GROUP B

Real Federacion Espanola de Futbol founded 1913. Joined FIFA 1904.

Previously qualified: 1964 (1st), 1980, 1984 (2nd) and 1988.

Present tournament Finished top of Group 2 with 26 points from 10 games ahead of
DENMARK (3-0 at home and 1-1 away)
BELGIUM (4-1 away and 1-1 at home)
CYPRUS (2-1 away and 6-0 at home)
MACEDONIA (2-0 away and 3-0 at home)
ARMENIA (2- 0 away and 1-0 at home)

The manager *Javier Clemente* (46) was a gifted midfielder whose career was cut short by injury. He coached Atletico Bilbao, where they won the League and Cup double in 1984, Atletico Madrid, and Bilbao (again) from 1990. He became manager after SPAIN failed to qualify for the 1992 European Championship. They won the 1992 Olympic title, however and having drafted in several of those players, SPAIN then reached the last eight in 1994. Clemente very strongly supports the ideals of playing a 4-4-2 system and asking midfielders to make quick counter-attacks. But while most countries are intent on playing less, tiring club football, SPAIN has just increased their first division to 22 teams! The season ends only thirteen days before the start of Euro 96.

The goalkeepers will be the experienced *Andoni Zubizaretta* (34), who first played in January 1985. His deputy is *Santiago Canizares* (26), now with Real Madrid.

The defence should be drawn from *Alberto Belsue* (28) or *Alberto Ferrer* (24 on 6 June) of Barcelona, who man-marks like a terrier and who played in the 1994 World Cup. *Rafael Alkorta* (27) of Real Madrid and *Abelardo* (26 on 19 April) of Barcelona, who played in the 1994 World Cup, have been recent selections. Others include the versatile *Miguel Nadal* (27) from Barcelona and *Miguel Lasa* (24) from Real Madrid.

In midfield have been *Julen Guerrero* (22) from Atletico Bilbao and Atletico Madrid's creative *Jose Luis Caminero* (28), both of whom played in the 1994 World Cup finals, and both of whom love to burst into the attack. Also available have been the combative *Juan Goicoechea* (30) and *Luis Enrique* (26 on 8 May of Real Madrid). Others who have been impressive have been *Sergi* (24) and *Fernando Hierro* (28) from Real Madrid, both of whom played in the 1994 World Cup.

In attack *Julio Salinas* (33) has the experience, although his days might be numbered. But others could be *Jose Amavisca* (25 on 19 June), *Fransisco Kiko* (24 on 26 April) from Atletico Madrid, *Alfonso* (23) from Real Betis, and *Raul* (19 on 27 June), from Real Madrid. Two selected players who have been naturalized are *Juan Pizzi* (28 on 7 June), who was born in Argentina, and *Donato* (33) who was born in Brazil.

The top scorer with 4 of the 25 goals was *Hierro*.

SPAIN raced through their campaign, qualifying easily. In the past they have often under-performed. Maybe they won't this time.

SWITZERLAND

GROUP A

Schweizerischer Fussballverbund founded 1895. Joined FIFA 1904.

Previously qualified: Never.

Present competition First in Group 3 with 17 points from 8 games
against
TURKEY (2-1 away and 1-2 at home)
SWEDEN (4-2 at home and 0-0 away)
HUNGARY (2-2 away and 3-0 at home)
ICELAND (1-0 at home and 2-0 away)

The manager *Roy Hodgson* (48) was once manager of Bristol City, and
later in Sweden with Halmstad and Malmo. He guided Malmo to five
championships (1985-90), before moving in 1990 to Xamax Neuchatel in
Switzerland. He started coaching SWITZERLAND on 1 January 1992 and
steered the country to the finals of the 1994 World Cup finals, the first
time since 1966. He followed this by guiding it to this European
Championship. It came as no surprise when in October 1995 he became
the technical director of Internazionale of Milan. Sadly, he was dismissed in
December 1995 and replaced by the Portuguese *Artur Jorge*, who has
coached Benfica and Paris Saint Germain.

The goalkeeper has been *Marco Pascolo* (32 on 22 May) with *Pascal
Zuberbuehler* (25) of Grasshopper Zurich as his deputy.

The defence has been drawn from *Alain Geiger* (35) as sweeper; at right-
back the overlapping *Marc Hottiger* (28), who joined Newcastle in 1994;
the immensely-promising *Stephane Henchoz* (22); *Dominque Herr* (30); with
Yvan Quentin (26 on 2 May) at left-back. *Ramon Vega* (25 on 4 June) of
Grasshopper and *Pascal Thueler* (26) are others who have played.

In midfield have been *Alain Sutter* (28) and *Ciriaco Sforza* (26) with his penetrative runs, who are with Bayern Munich. *Christophe Orhel* (28 on 7 April); the left-footed *Thomas Bickel* (32); *Sebastien Fournier* (25 on 27 June), who was in the team in Sweden; and his club colleague at Sion, *Christophe Bonvin* (31 on 14 April), are others who have played. *Murat Yakin* (21) is a player of great promise.

In the attack have been the opportunist *Adrian Knup* (28 on 2 July) of Karlsruhe and the prolific *Stefan Chapuisat* (27 on 28 June), who plays with the German champions Borussia Dortmund. Others include the Argentine-born *Nestor Subiat* (30 on 23 April) of Grasshopper, who scored two late goals in HUNGARY, and the opportunist *Kubilay Turkilmaz* (29) of Galatasaray, who was born in the Italian part of Switzerland to Turkish parents. *Marco Grassi* (27) with Rennes in France is a player of great potential.

The top goal-scorer was *Turkilmaz* with 3 of the 15 goals, *Bickel*, *Ohrel*, *Sforza* and *Subiat* scored 2.

The recent record of SWITZERLAND is astonishing for a small country. And it comes as no surprise that many of their midfield and attacking stars play for teams in the classy German Bundesliga.

TURKEY

GROUP D

Turkiye Futbol Federasyonu founded 1923. Joined FIFA 1923.

Previously qualified: Never.

Present tournament Second in Group 3 with 15 points from 8 matches behind SWITZERLAND (1-2 at home and 2-1 away) but ahead of
SWEDEN (2-1 at home and 2-2 away)
HUNGARY (2-2 away and 2-0 at home)
ICELAND (5-0 at home and 0-0 away)

The manager The man responsible for steering TURKEY to their first appearance in a major championship since the 1954 World Cup has been *Faith Terim* (41). A previous captain (35 times) and record-holder for number of appearances (51) for TURKEY, he took over from the Dane *Sepp Piontek* in August 1993, converting his 3-5-2 to a 3-4-2-1 formation.

The goalkeepers have been *Engin Ipekoglu* (35 on 7 June) and *Rustu Recber* (23 on 1 May).

The defence will see *Bulent Korkmaz* (28) of Galatasaray and *Ogun Temizkanoglu* (27 on 10 June) at centre-back, with *Gokhan Keskin* (30) as sweeper. *Recep Cetin* (30) plays at right-back. Others who have played include *Emre Asik* (22), *Alpay Ozolan* (24), *Tayfur Havuteu* (18), and the experienced *Yusuf Tepekule* (27) from Galatasaray.

The midfield has the goal-scoring and goal-making *Bulent Yugun* (24); *Abdullah Evcan* (24); and the experienced *Oguz Cetin* (33) of Fenerbahce. He was first chosen to play in a 'peace' match against GREECE in

September 1988, and went on to break Terim's record for number of appearances. *Suat Kaya* (28) of Galatasaray has been on outstanding form; others who have played are *Sergen Yalcin* (24); the highly-gifted *Tugay Kerimoglu* (25); the recently-capped *Okan Buruk* (22); and *Abdullah Ercan* (24).

The attack will have the tall *Hakan Sukur* (24), who returned to Galatasaray after playing only five games for Torino because of his homesickness for Istanbul. Indeed, in the home match against HUNGARY, he scored both goals. His colleagues have included the lively *Saffet Sancakli* (30); *Ertugrul Saghlam* (26) of Besiktas, and *Hami Mondirali* (28 on 6 June).

The top scorer with 7 of the 16 goals was *Hakan*.

Whatever happens in June, *Faith Terim* is looking forward to inspiring another triumphant qualification. This time for the 1998 World Cup Finals!

SOME OF THE LEADING STARS

ABDULLAH Ercan (Turkey). Born 8 December 1971. He's a blond-haired left-sided midfield player who plays for Trabzonspor. For both his club side and the national team, he has been on excellent form, using his fluent skills to create scoring opportunities for his team-mates.

Tony ADAMS (England). Born 10 October 1966. He has been the long-serving stopper with Arsenal, with whom he has won numerous trophies including two titles and the 1993/94 Cup-Winners' Cup. He was first chosen for England in February 1987, played in the 1988 tournament, and after being reserve to Des Walker, has regained his place.

Demetrio ALBERTINI (Italy). Born 23 August 1971. He's a central midfielder who was loaned to Padua for the 1990/91 season, but since then has benefited considerably from experience of playing in European competitions with A.C. Milan. He starred in the 1994 World Cup finals, and scored the vital goal in the 1-1 draw in Croatia.

Rafael ALKORTA (Spain). Born 16 September 1969. He's a swift central defender. He started his career with Atletico Bilbao before moving in 1993 to Real Madrid. With them he's been getting valuable European experience, particularly in the recent Champions League. He played in the 1994 World Cup finals.

Darren ANDERTON (England). Born 3 March 1972. He's a graceful winger who was signed from Portsmouth for Spurs by Terry Venables in

1992. He has played regularly for England since gaining his first cap against Denmark in March 1994, and could be an influential player in June.

Jocelyn **ANGLOMA** (France). Born 7 August 1965. He's a fluid right-back who moved from Paris Saint-Germain to Olympique Marseille in the summer of 1991. He was in the side that won the European Cup in 1993, but when OM were then punished with relegation for making bribes, in 1994 moved to Torino. He played in the 1992 European Championship.

Dino **BAGGIO** (Italy). Born 24 July 1971. He's a tough midfielder, a modern-day Marco Tardelli, who started with Torino, moved to Inter, and in 1994 moved from Juventus to Parma. He played outstandingly in US 1994, scoring the only goal in the match against Norway and the first in the 2-1 win against Spain.

Roberto **BAGGIO** (Italy). Born 18 February 1967. He's an attacking midfield player who is sheer class, and is fearsome with free kicks. In 1990 he was transferred from Fiorentina to Juventus, whom he helped to win the UEFA Cup in 1993 - the year he was elected European Footballer of the Year. After helping Juventus gain the league title for 1994/95, he was allowed to leave for A.C. Milan. He gained his first cap in November 1988, and during the 1990 World Cup scored a memorable goal against Czechoslovakia. Although carrying an injury to a tendon, Baggio was outstanding in the 1994 World Cup. He scored sensational goals against Nigeria, Spain and Bulgaria, and did much to help an extremely lucky Italy finish as runners-up.

Vitor **BAIA** (Portugal). Born 15 October 1969. He first played for Porto when he was only 20, and his assured goalkeeping has helped them to be in European competitions for the last seven seasons. He has been a permanent fixture in Portugal's team since 1991, and could be one of the best players in the competition.

Krasimir **BALAKOV** (Bulgaria). Born 29 March 1966. A midfielder who's most powerful running forward, he joined Sporting Lisbon in 1991, and in 1995 moved to VB Stuttgart. He had an outstanding tournament in the 1994 World Cup finals, did much to ensure that Bulgaria finished fourth, and was voted a member of the All-Star Team.

John **BARNES** (England). Born 7 November 1963. The gifted Barnes, now with Liverpool, is an astute passer of the ball who was first selected in May 1983 when he was with Watford. He took part in the World Cups of 1986 and 1990 and the European Championships of 1988, but injury prevented him from playing in 1992.

Mario **BASLER** (Germany). Born 18 December 1968. 'Super Mario' is a right-sided midfield player who has all the skills (inswinging corners, deadly free kicks and pin-point passes among them). In 1993 he moved from Hertha Berlin to Werder Bremen. He was first selected in March 1994, and played one game in US 1994.

Miodrag **BELODEDIC** (Rumania). Born 20 May 1964. A most elegant defender, he played for Steaua Bucharest, who won the European Cup in 1986. In January 1989 he sought asylum in Serbia (where he was born), played for Red Star Belgrade, was later transferred to Valencia and then Valladolid. He played in the 1994 World Cup finals.

Alberto **BELSUE** (Spain). Born 2 March 1968. He is a fast, hard-working right-back, whose performances for Real Zaragoza have been outstanding. His fine form earned him his call-up for the national side. He first represented them in November 1994, and broke up the full-back partnership of Ferrer and Sergi.

Patrik **BERGER** (Czech Republic). Born 10 November 1973. A talented left-sided midfielder, in 1995 he was transferred by Slavia Prague to

Borussia Dortmund. With them he is gaining valuable experience in the Champions League, and continues to score fine goals.

Dennis BERGKAMP (Holland). Born 10 May 1969. A swift, lithe central attacker who is expert at losing defenders, Bergkamp moved from Ajax to Internazionale-Milan in 1993. But he was unable to settle and moved on to Arsenal in June 1995 and returned to scoring goals. He gained his first cap soon after Italia 90, and came to wider prominence during the 1992 European Championship. He then starred in the 1994 World Cup finals.

Slaven BILIC (Croatia). Born 11 September 1968. He is a key central defender who is outstanding in the air. He started his career with Hajduk Split, in 1993 moved to Karlsruhe in Germany, and in December 1995 to West Ham United.

Laurent BLANC (France). Born 19 November 1965. A former midfield player, Blanc is an attack-minded *libero* who moved from Montpellier to Napoli in June 1991. He failed to settle however, moved back to St Etienne, and in 1995 moved to Auxerre. He played in the 1992 European Championships.

Zvonimir BOBAN (Croatia). Born 8 October 1969. He's an outstandingly creative midfield player who used to play for Dynamo Zagreb. He moved to Italy in 1991, and after a spell with Bari is presently with A.C. Milan. His experience was a vital factor in ensuring that Croatia finished top of their group.

Frank de BOER (Holland). Born 15 May 1970. He's a fine centre-back, whose performances were outstanding when Ajax Amsterdam gained the European Cup and the Inter-Continental Cup for the 1994/95 season. First selected in September 1990, he played in the 1992 tournament, as well as US 1994. Twin of club-colleague Ronald, his ambition is 'to win everything at least once'.

Alen BOKSIC [Croatia]. Born 21 January 1970. A tall central striker, he moved from Hajduk Split to Olympique Marseille in 1991. He scored prolifically in the 1992/93 season, helped them win the European Cup in 1993, and then moved to Lazio in November 1993. He hasn't done himself justice for Croatia. Yet . . .

Scott BOOTH (Scotland). Born 16 December 1971. He is a newly-capped and exciting striker from Aberdeen who scored the decisive single goal in the home tie with Finland. Together with his club mate, Eion Jess, he could form a crucial role in Scotland's plans.

Jorge Paulo CADETTE (Portugal). Born 27 August 1968. He's a fast-moving central striker who, after starting in midfield, was encouraged to play as a forward during the 1989/90 season. He joined Brescia from Sporting Lisbon in November 1994, before returning there in 1995. First selected on 5 September 1990.

Jose Luis CAMINERO (Spain). Born 8 November 1967. He's a midfield star who once was rejected by Real Madrid, and in 1993 joined Atletico Madrid from Valladolid. He had an inspired tournament in US 1994, although he had been plagued by injury in the months before.

Eric CANTONA (France). Born 24 May 1966. A skilful and tempestuous player, he joined Leeds United in 1991 and helped it win the League title, then joined Manchester United. So far he has helped them win three League titles and triumph in the 1994 F.A. Cup. No wonder Alex Ferguson refers to him as 'mon genius'. He played in the 1992 European Championship, and France could make good use of his skills.

Stephane CHAPUISAT (Switzerland). Born 28 June 1969. A most talented striker, who is with Borussia Dortmund in Germany. There he has proved he could score against tight defences. He played in the 1994 World Cup finals, but knee ligament damage in early 1995 saw him miss playing for the following ten months.

John COLLINS (Scotland). Born 31 July 1968. He's an intelligent midfield player who frequently scores goals, and has a splendid free kick. Transferred from Hibernian to Glasgow Celtic in 1990 he's also gaining European experience at club level alongside Paul McStay.

Fernando COUTO (Portugal). Born 2 August 1969. He's a tall, well-built centre-back who joined Parma from Porto in the middle of 1994 after four highly successful seasons.

Edgar DAVIDS (Holland). Born 13 March 1973. He is an attacking midfield player who makes cool interceptions and passes outstandingly. With Ajax in 1995 he won the European Cup and the Intercontinental Cup. He has performed eminently for Holland, playing particularly well in the play-off match.

Alessandro DEL PIERO (Italy). Born 9 November 1974. He's a most exciting midfield player who did much to win Juventus the title in 1994/95. An expert with free kicks, he brings back memories of Michel Platini; and, playing alongside Fabrizio Ravanelli, has scored some truly exciting goals.

Marcel DESAILLY (France). Born 7 September 1968. After spells with Nantes and Marseille, in 1993 he joined A.C. Milan, and helped it win the European Champions' Cup in May 1994. He's a versatile player either in midfield or the defence, as shown by the fact that in France's final match he played as stopper!

Didier DESCHAMPS (France). Born 15 October 1968. He's an authoritative midfield player who started with Nantes, was then transferred to Olympique Marseille, and then Bordeaux. In 1994 he moved to Juventus, and helped them become champions. He's an experienced international who played in the 1992 tournament.

Youri DJORKAEFF (France). Born 9 March 1968. An attacking midfield player, he joined AS Monaco in 1991, and moved to Paris Saint Germain in 1995. First selected by Aimé Jacquet in February 1994, he scored the goal when France beat Italy 1-0 in Naples, and his five qualifying goals came in the final four matches.

Igor DOBROVOLSKI (USSR). Born 27 August 1967. He has played for sides in Spain, Switzerland, Italy, France and Spain (again), but now has returned to Moscow Dynamo, clearly never able to settle happily abroad. Dobrovolski shone as a midfield star in the final stages of the 1990 World Cup and the 1992 European Championship.

Radek DRULAK (Czech Republic). Born 12 January 1962. He's a lively central striker who plays for Petra Drnovice. He scored a crucial second goal in the home game against Norway. His two goals against Luxembourg in the final game ensured that the Czech Republic finished top of their group.

Ilie DUMITRESCU (Rumania). Born 6 January 1969. A fine midfielder who moved from Steaua Bucharest to Tottenham Hotspur in 1994, was loaned to Seville, and now has rejoined Spurs, although used sparingly. He teams up well with Hagi, and always looks for a chance to score. He played in the 1990 and 1994 World Cup finals.

Albert FERRER (Spain). Born 6 June 1970. He's a speedy right-back who marks as tight as a limpet. Playing for Barcelona provides additional European experience. After gaining a gold medal at the 1992 Olympic Games he was a regular fixture in Javier Clemente's sides, and played in the 1994 World Cup finals.

Paulo FUTRE (Portugal). Born 1 March 1965. He's a most exciting forward with a magical left foot. After spells with Atletico Madrid, he moved to Benfica, Marseille and Reggiana before joining A.C. Milan in

1995. He played in the 1986 World Cup finals, but sadly injuries have checkered his career.

Paul GASCOIGNE (England). Born 24 May 1967. He's a midfielder with rare talent who was purchased by Terry Venables for Tottenham Hotspur from Newcastle United. But an injury to the ligaments in his right knee during the 1991 Cup Final postponed his proposed move to Lazio, and he was unable to take part in the final stages of the 1992 European Championship. His three-year spell in Italy failed to display his full talents, however, because in April 1994 he broke his right leg and was out of the game for another ten months. He joined Glasgow Rangers in 1995. But his performances in the 1990 World Cup did much to gain England fourth place. He started his first international under Terry Venables with an inspiring performance against Colombia in September 1995.

Alain GEIGER (Switzerland). Born 5 November 1960. He's an experienced sweeper who played for Sion, Servette, Neuchatel Xamax, and Saint-Etienne in France, before returning to Sion in 1990, and moved on to Grasshopper in 1995. An ever-present choice, the 1994 World Cup finals saw him gain his 100th selection.

David GINOLA (France). Born 25 January 1967. He's a most exciting left-footed forward. In 1995 he joined Newcastle United from Paris Saint Germain whom he had helped win the 1993/94 championship. A player of great flair, his skills could be vital to the success of France, and with Newcastle he has increased his commitment.

Andy GORAM (Scotland). Born 13 April 1964. He's an excellent goalkeeper who moved in 1987 from Oldham to Hibernian, and in 1991 from Hibernian to Rangers, for whom he has been on outstanding form. First chosen in 1985, he played in all three of Scotland's matches in the 1992 European Championship.

Gheorghe HAGI (Rumania). Born 5 February 1965. Among the most inventive midfield players in Europe, he was transferred to Real Madrid, joined Brescia in 1992, and Barcelona in 1994. He first played in Rumania's side in 1984, and featured in the World Cup finals of 1990 and 1994 finals.

HAKAN Sukur (Turkey). Born 1 September 1971. The tall Hakan knew great success with his club, Galatasaray, between 1992 and 1995. His time in Italy in late 1995 was brief, since he returned after playing only five games for Torino because of his homesickness for Istanbul. But he has regained his threatening form.

Thomas HASSLER (Germany). Born 30 May 1966. He's a right-sided midfield player who was transferred from Cologne to Juventus in 1990, in 1991 moved south to Roma, and in 1994 back to Karlsruhe. He was out-standing in the 1992 European Nations Championship; he scored Germany's first and equalising goal in the last minute of the match against CIS with a curling free kick. He played in the 1990 and 1994 World Cup finals.

Thomas HELMER (Germany). Born 21 April 1965. A versatile defender, in 1992 he was transferred from Borussia Dortmund to Bayern Munich. He replaced Manfred Binz in the role of sweeper during the 1992 European Nations Championship, and played in the 1994 World Cup finals.

Stephane HENCHOZ (Switzerland). Born 7 September 1974. He's a centre back who was transferred by Neuchatel Xamax to Hamburg in 1995. He failed to make the 1994 World Cup squad, but recently has been chosen regularly.

Dominique HERR (Switzerland). Born 25 October 1965. He's a left back or central defender who gained his first selection in September 1989, and has been a virtual ever-present since then. He played in the 1994 World Cup finals.

Heiko **HERRLICH** (Germany). Born 3 December 1971. He's an exciting central striker who was transferred from Borussia Moenchengladbach, and plays for Borussia Dortmund. He was first capped in March 1995 and is living up to the translation of his name as 'magnificent'.

Fernando **HIERRO** (Spain). Born 23 March 1968. He's a hard-running midfield player who started his career with Real Valladolid before moving to Real Madrid in 1989, the year he was first selected. He scored the goal in the 1-0 victory over Denmark that assured Spain of qualification, and played in the 1994 World Cup finals.

Marc **HOTTIGER** (Switzerland). Born 7 November 1967. He's a fluent right-back who played in the 1994 World Cup finals, after which he was transferred from F.C. Sion to Newcastle United.

John **JENSEN** (Denmark). Born 3 May 1965. He is an industrious and skilful midfield player who moved from Brondby to Arsenal in 1992. He won the Cup-Winners' Cup for Arsenal in 1993/94, and was a finalist last year. He has been a regular member of Denmark's side, including the victorious team in 1992.

Andrei **KANCHELSKIS** (Russia). Born 23 January 1969. This fleet-footed winger joined Manchester United in May 1991, helped them become champions in 1993 and 1994, and in 1995 moved to Everton. He took part in the 1992 European Championship, where he was used as right-back, but refused to play in the 1994 World Cup finals.

Christian **KAREMBEU** (France). Born 3 December 1970. He's an exciting midfield player who in 1995 moved to Sampdoria from Nantes, whom he'd helped win the League. First chosen in November 1992, he is part of a most impressive French midfield.

Dmitri KHARIN (Russia). Born 16 August 1968. An agile goalkeeper, he was transferred to Chelsea in 1992, for whom he has been showing outstanding form. First chosen for the USSR in 1990, he took part for the CIS in the European Championship of 1992, and Russia in the 1994 World Cup finals.

Petar KHUBCHEV (Bulgaria). Born 26 February 1964. Bought by Levski Sofia in 1989, then in 1993 by SV Hamburger (where he plays with Yordan Letchkov), Khubchev is a sweeper of great poise. He played outstandingly in the 1994 World Cup finals.

Sergei KIRIAKOV (Russia). Born 1 January 1970. He's a lithe forward who took part in the 1992 European Championship, after which he joined Karlsruhe in Germany. He refused to play in the 1994 World Cup finals, but scored three goals in the Euro 96 qualifying tournament, and will be a player to watch.

Jurgen KLINSMANN (Germany). Born 30 July 1964. A tall, lithe central striker who joined Internazionale of Milan from Stuttgart in 1989, and settled in most effectively. In 1992 he moved to Monaco, and in 1994 joined Tottenham Hotspur. But after an enormously successful year he returned to Germany and Bayern Munich, for whom he has been prolific. He played in the 1988 European Championship, and his majestic forward play did much to make West Germany triumph in the 1990 World Cup. He took part in the 1992 European Championship, and scored five goals in the 1994 World Cup, when he was one of the few German successes. This outstanding form continued during the qualifying campaign for Euro 96.

Patrick KLUIVERT (Holland). Born 1 July 1976. He is a wonderfully talented central striker who scored the only goal when Ajax Amsterdam gained the European Cup for the 1994/95 season. He also scored both goals when Holland beat the Republic of Ireland 2-0 in the play-off eliminator in December 1995.

Adrian KNUP (Switzerland). Born 2 July 1968. An experienced and fine striker who has played with Basel, Aarau and Lucerne. But in 1992 he moved to Germany with Stuttgart, and in 1994 joined Karlsruhe. A prolific scorer, he played in the 1994 World Cup, and combines well with the pacy Kubilay Turkilmaz.

Jurgen KOHLER (Germany). Born 6 October 1965. An outstanding central defender who was transferred in June 1991 from Bayern Munich to Juventus, whom he helped to win the UEFA Cup in 1991 and 1993, and the league title in 1995. In 1995 he joined Borussia Dortmund, the champions of Germany. He did much to help West Germany win the 1990 World Cup, and took part in the 1992 European Championship and the 1994 World Cup.

Igor KOLYVANOV (Russia). Born 6 March 1968. He's a fast-moving and skilful central attacker who now represents Foggia in Italy. He played for the CIS in the 1992 European Championship, but refused to represent Russia in the 1994 World Cup.

Emil KOSTADINOV (Bulgaria). Born 12 August 1967. He's a pacy forward who was transferred by CSKA Sofia to Porto during 1990, and now is with Bayern Munich. In November 1993 he scored the winning goal only 10 seconds from the final whistle against France, thereby paving the way to a memorable World Cup 1994.

Pavel KUKA (Czech Republic). Born 19 July 1968. He's a gifted attacker. In 1994 he joined Kaiserslautern from Slavia Prague,whom he had joined in 1989. First selected in 1991, he has been a regular member of the national team ever since.

Marius **LACATUS** (Rumania). Born 5 April 1964. He was a member of Steaua Bucharest, who won the European Cup in 1986. After that he was signed by Fiorentina, and moved on to Oviedo in Spain, but now has returned to Steaua. He scored spectacular goals in the 1990 World Cup, and has regained his place in the national side.

Bernard **LAMA** (France). Born 17 April 1963. A brave goalkeeper, he presently plays with Paris Saint Germain. whom he joined in 1992 from Lens. The French defence in this tournament played 575 minutes before it conceded a goal, the goalkeeper responsible for this being Lama. He won his first cap in February 1993.

Graeme **LE SAUX** (England). Born 17 October 1968. A left-sided player he was transferred to Blackburn Rovers by Chelsea in 1993 and is an excellent crosser after his long runs. He was in the first side chosen by Terry Venables in March 1994, and was an ever-present until he dislocated his right ankle in December 1995.

Brian **LAUDRUP** (Denmark). Born 22 February 1969. He's a sparkling inside-forward who was transferred from Brondby to Fiorentina in 1992, moved to A.C. Milan in 1993, and in 1994 to Rangers, where he teamed up fluently with Paul Gascoigne. His displays in the 1992 tournament were instrumental in gaining the title for his country.

Michael **LAUDRUP** (Denmark). Born 15 June 1964. A most gifted forward, he was transferred in 1983 from Brondby to Juventus. In Italy he played two seasons with Lazio and four with Juventus. He then moved to join Johan Cruyff at Barcelona in 1989, and in 1995 to Real Madrid. He took part in the final stages of the 1984 and 1988 European Championships, as well as the 1986 World Cup, but refused to play for Richard Moller-Nielsen. That rift has now been mended, and he played a crucial role behind the front two in the Euro 96 qualifying round.

Yordan LETCHKOV (Bulgaria). Born 9 July 1967. A former striker, he dropped back to midfield after his transfer in 1992 from CSKA Sofia to SV Hamburg in Germany. First chosen in October 1989, he played outstandingly in the 1994 World Cup finals, and scored the goal that eliminated Germany.

Gary McALLISTER (Scotland). Born 25 December 1964. He's an inside-forward who in 1985 moved from Motherwell to Leicester City, and in 1990 to Leeds United, whom he steered to win the League in 1992. In that year he was also outstanding in the European Championship, and continues to be most influential.

Steve McMANAMAN (England). Born 11 February 1972. His scintillating running helped Liverpool win the F.A. Cup for 1992. Further exciting displays eventually paved the way for his entry into international football. This came against Nigeria in November 1994.

Paolo MALDINI (Italy). Born 26 June 1968. The popular Maldini is a polished left-back who has been one of the mainstays of the victorious A.C. Milan defence for the last few seasons. First chosen in March 1988, he played outstandingly in the 1988 European Championship, as well as in the 1990 and 1994 World Cup finals.

Borislav MIKHAILOV (Bulgaria). Born 12 February 1962. First selected as goalkeeper in 1964, he's the most experienced of Bulgaria's players. He took part in the 1986 World Cup, and was most impressive in 1994 World Cup finals. His daily life is much less pressured: for Reading, whom he joined from Botev Plovdiv.

Andreas MOELLER (Germany). Born 2 September 1967. A midfield player, he moved from Eintracht Frankfurt to Juventus in 1992, and in 1994 to Borussia Dortmund. He played as a substitute in the 1990 World Cup, but took part fully in the finals of the 1992 European Championship, and the 1994 World Cup finals.

Miguel Angel NADAL (Spain). Born 28 July 1966. He's a central defender or utility player who was first selected in 1992 and played in the 1994 World Cup finals. Playing his club football for Barcelona has provided him with much international experience.

Yuri NIKIFOROV (Russia). Born 16 September 1970. He's an outstanding sweeper who played in all three of Russia's matches during the 1994 World Cup finals. He now plays for Spartak Moscow, whom he joined in 1993.

Viktor ONOPKO (Russia). Born 14 October 1969. A Ukrainian, he's a versatile defender who moved to Spartak Moscow in 1992. He played in the 1992 European Championships, has since been a regular choice, played impressively in the 1994 World Cup finals, and moved to Atletico Madrid in December 1995.

Liuboslov PENEV (Bulgaria). Born 31 August 1966. He's a central attacker who joined Valencia in late 1989 from CSKA Sofia. He now plays for Atletico Madrid, for whom he has been on prolific form.

Dan PETRESCU (Rumania). Born 22 December 1967. He's a gifted right back who moved from Steaua Bucharest to Foggia in 1991, and then to Genoa in 1993. He was transferred to Sheffield Wednesday in 1994, and in October 1995 moved to Chelsea. He played in the 1994 World Cup finals.

David PLATT (England). Born 10 June 1965. He's undoubtedly one of the foremost midfield players in the world. First capped against Italy in November 1989, he replaced Bryan Robson in England's match with Holland during the 1990 World Cup and proceeded to score three goals, none more vital than that against Belgium in the final minute of extra time, which helped England proceed to the quarter final against Cameroon and the semi-final against West Germany. He played in the 1992 European Championship. In July 1991 he was sold by Aston Villa to Bari for a record sum of £5,500,000, moved a year later to Juventus, and in 1993 to Sampdoria - finally returning to England and Arsenal in 1995.

Gica POPESCU (Rumania). Born 9 October 1967. In 1990 he moved from Universitatea Craiova to PSV Eindhoven, and in 1994 to Tottenham Hotspur. In May 1995 he was transferred to Barcelona, where he has been on fine form. He played outstandingly as sweeper during the 1990 World Cup finals, and in midfield four years later.

Robert PROSINECKI (Croatia). Born 12 January 1969. He was transferred by Red Star Belgrade, with whom he won the 1991 European Cup, to Real Madrid in 1992. In 1995 he joined Barcelona. He was used sparingly during the 1990 World Cup, but has since become one of the notable midfield players in Europe.

Dmitri RADCHENKO (Russia). Born 2 December 1970. He's an attacking player who took part in all three of Russia's games in the 1994 World Cup finals, and scored the sixth goal in the 6-1 defeat of Cameroon. In 1995 he moved from Racing Santander to Deportivo La Coruna.

Florin RADUCIOU (Rumania). Born 17 March 1970. Raduciou is a striker who was transferred from Dinamo Bucharest to Bari in 1990. Then followed spells with Verona, Brescia, and A.C. Milan, before he moved on to Espanol. He took part in the 1990 World Cup finals, and in the 1994 World Cup he scored four goals.

Karlheinz RIEDLE (Germany). Born 9 September 1965. An outstanding header of a ball, Riedle moved from Werder Bremen to Lazio in 1990. In 1993 was transferred to Borussia Dortmund, who won the 1994/95 title. He played in the 1990 and 1994 World Cup finals, and the 1992 European Championship.

Marc RIEPER (Denmark). Born 5 June 1968. Rieper is a strong centre back who was signed from Brondby for West Ham United during 1994. He was first chosen for Denmark in 1991, although he took no part in the Danish triumph in 1992. He has now formed a strong partnership with Chelsea's Jacob Kjeldbjerg.

Manuel RUI COSTA (Portugal). Born 29 March 1972. He's a superb inside-forward who in 1994 joined Fiorentina after three seasons with Benfica. He was first chosen in March 1993, and scored the crucial opening goal with a superb 25-metre chip in the 3-0 defeat of Ireland in Lisbon.

Julio SALINAS (Spain). Born 11 September 1962. He is a most experienced forward who spent many seasons with Barcelona, and in 1995 left Deportivo for Sporting Gijon. He played in the 1986, 1990 and 1994 World Cup finals, and the 1988 European Championship. Will he be needed again?

Mattias SAMMER (Germany). Born 5 September 1967. Sammer was the first player from East Germany to be selected for the complete German team when the two parts of Germany unified in late 1990. A driving midfield player who originally played for Dynamo Dresden, in 1990 he was transferred to Stuttgart, and in 1992 joined Internazionale. He was played disastrously out of position and in December returned to Germany and Borussia Dortmund, with whom he won the 1994/95 title. He took part in the 1992 European Championships and the 1994 World Cup finals.

Paulinho SANTOS (Portugal). Born 21 November 1970. He's a left-sided defender with Porto, the team managed by former England manager Bobby Robson. First chosen in January 1994, Paulinho Santos could be one of the outstanding players of the tournament.

Peter SCHMEICHEL (Denmark). Born 18 November 1961. A most experienced goalkeeper who was transferred in June 1991 from Brondby to

Manchester United, and helped it win the League title for 1992, 1993, 1994. He played in the 1988 European finals, and the victorious side in 1992.

Carlos **SECRETARIO** (Portugal). Born 12 May 1970. Secretario is a wing-back with Porto who loves to set up attacks. First selected in December 1994, he is rapidly establishing his place in the national team.

SERGI (Spain). Born 28 December 1971. Sergi Barijuan is a left-sided defender who burst into the Barcelona team in 1993. In fact he played so well that he gained his first cap just before the 1994 World Cup finals. In these he was excellent.

Ciriaco **SFORZA** (Switzerland). Born 2 March 1970. Sforza is an outstanding playmaker, who has a fierce free kick. In March 1995 he moved from Kaiserslautern to Bayern Munich. First selected in August 1990, he played in the 1994 World Cup finals, and scored the goal against Hungary that helped Switzerland to qualify.

Igor **SHALIMOV** (Soviet Union). Born 2 February 1969. Shalimov is a versatile midfielder who makes telling runs into the attack. In July 1991 he left Moscow Spartak for Foggia, for whom he had a magnificent season. A year later he was transferred to Internazionale-Milan, who in 1994 loaned him to Lugano, and in 1995 to Udinese. First selected in May 1990, Shalimov played in World Cup 1990, and in the 1992 European Championships, although he refused to play in the 1994 World Cup. He could be one of the most skilful players on view.

Alan **SHEARER** (England). Born 13 August 1970. He was transferred from Southampton to Blackburn Rovers, with whom he became England's top scorer in 1994/95 season. He played in the 1992 European Nations Championship, but injury soon after seriously damaged England's chances of qualifying for the 1994 World Cup.

Giuseppe SIGNORI (Italy). Born 17 February 1968. He is a pacy left-footed striker who in 1992 moved from Foggia to Lazio, and was the top scorer in Italy for the 1992/93 and 1993/94 seasons. He played in the 1994 World Cup finals, and Italy needs him at his best.

Tomas SKHURAVY (Czech Republic). Born 7 September 1965. The tall Skhuravy joined Genoa from Sparta Prague after the 1990 World Cup finals, and in 1995 moved to Sporting Lisbon. He has recently formed a good striking partnership with Pavel Kuka.

Paolo SOUSA (Portugal). Born 3 August 1970. An elegant midfield playmaker from deep positions, he spent four seasons with Benfica, one with Sporting Lisbon. He has just finished his second season with Juventus. First selected in 1992, he was outstanding in the Euro 96 qualifying competition.

Hristo STOICHKOV (Bulgaria). Born 11 September 1966. Stoichkov is the greatest footballer his country has produced, and won the European Player for 1994. He shared the Golden Boot trophy for having scored most goals in 1989-90 while he was with C.S.K.A. Sofia, after which he moved to the new Spanish champions, Barcelona, for whom he was a prolific scorer, alongside the brilliant Brazilian, Romario. His six goals brought another shared Golden Boot trophy and helped Bulgaria to be semi-finalists in the 1994 World Cup, but in 1995 he moved to Parma.

Steve STONE (England). Born 20 August 1971. The 24-year-old wide midfield player has been on outstanding form for Nottingham Forest, whom he joined in 1991. He made an excellent debut against Switzerland in November 1994, making one goal and scoring another, and played with great maturity.

Davor **SUKER** (Croatia). Born 1 January 1968. He's a lethal finisher inside the box and plays for Seville, whom he joined from Dinamo Zagreb in 1991. The civil war ruined his chances of appearing on the international stage, but he signified his intent by becoming the leading scorer in the Euro 96 qualifying competition.

Sergei **YURAN** (Russia). Born 11 June 1969. He's a prolific goalscorer who in 1991 left Dinamo Kiev for Benfica. In July 1995, however, he left to rejoin Moscow Spartak, for whom he scores important goals. He played in the 1992 tournament for the CIS, and the 1994 World Cup for Russia.

Christian **ZIEGE** (Germany). Born 1 February 1972. He is a most impressive 'wing back' with Bayern Munich. He was first selected in 1993 and was hailed as a new star after playing outstandingly in the US Cup in 1993. He was injured just before the 1994 World Cup finals, and his absence was critical.

Gianfranco **ZOLA** (Italy). Born 5 July 1966. This gloriously skilful Corsican attacking inside-forward player started his career with Napoli. There his skills during the 1991/92 season meant that Diego Maradona was barely missed. But it was following his transfer to Parma in 1993 that his game improved markedly. His generalship did much to gain Parma the Supercup in 1994. He was first chosen in November 1991, and played in the 1994 World Cup. He is now a central figure in the Italian national team.

Andoni **ZUBIZARRETA** (Spain). Born 23 October 1961. An outstanding goalkeeper who started with Atletico Bilbao, but was purchased in 1985 by Terry Venables for Barcelona, and helped it win League titles and various Cups. In 1994 he moved to Valencia. He made his international debut in January 1985, and played in the World Cup finals of 1986, 1990 and 1994, and the European Championships of 1988.

STATISTICS AND CURIOSITIES

The **first match** in the history of the tournament took place on 5 April 1959 when the REPUBLIC OF IRELAND beat CZECHOSLOVAKIA 2-0 in Dublin. A knock-out formula had been agreed on, but since 17 teams had entered for the 1960 finals, it was necessary to play a decider to see who should continue. Czechoslovakia, who won the return match 4-0, went on to finish third.

The **first goal** was scored by *Liam Tuohy* (REPUBLIC OF IRELAND).

The **first player to be dismissed** was *Alan Mullery* during ENGLAND's 1-0 defeat by YUGOSLAVIA in June 1968 for a retaliatory foul. But *Trivic* could have won an Oscar for his acting.

The **first five European Championships were won by different countries** - SOVIET UNION (1960), SPAIN (1964), ITALY (1968), WEST GERMANY (1972) and CZECHOSLOVAKIA (1976).

In 1980 WEST GERMANY became the **first to win it twice** by beating BELGIUM.

The **biggest attendance** came in the 1964 final in Madrid when on 21 June SPAIN defeated USSR 2-1 watched by a crowd of 120,000.

The **first ever clash between the reigning World Champions and European Champions** took place at the quarter-final stage of the 1968 tournament when ENGLAND defeated SPAIN 1-0 at Wembley and 2-1 in Madrid.

The final four matches in the 1976 tournament each had to be **decided after extra time**.

And the **final** itself was the **first to be decided after a penalty shoot-out** when CZECHOSLOVAKIA defeated WEST GERMANY 5-3 after the drawn match had finished 2-2.

In 1980 CZECHOSLOVAKIA also won after a penalty shoot-out when they beat ITALY 9-8 (after a 1-1 draw) to finish third.

The following scored **hat-tricks during the finals:**

1976 *Dieter Muller* (West Germany v Yugoslavia)

1980 *Klaus Allofs* (West Germany v Holland)

1984 *Michel Platini* (France v Yugoslavia)

1988 *Marco Van Basten* (Holland v England)

The **most individual goals** in the final stages of a single tournament were by *Michel Platini* who during five matches scored nine of FRANCE's fourteen goals in 1984.

LEADING SCORERS

	PLAYERS	GOALS	COUNTRY
1960	IVANOV AND PONEDELNIK	2	SOVIET UNION
	GALIC AND JERKOVIC	2	YUGOSLAVIA
	HEUTTE	2	FRANCE
1964	PEREDA	2	SPAIN
	NOVAK	2	HUNGARY
1968	DZAJIC	2	YUGOSLAVIA
1972	GERD MULLER	4	WEST GERMANY
1976	DIETER MULLER	4	WEST GERMANY
1980	KLAUS ALLOFS	3	WEST GERMANY
1984	PLATINI	9	FRANCE
1988	VAN BASTEN	5	HOLLAND
1992	LARSEN	3	DENMARK
	RIEDLE	3	GERMANY
	BERGKAMP	3	HOLLAND
	BROLIN	3	SWEDEN

PREVIOUS SUCCESSES

	1	2	3	4
1960	SOVIET UNION	YUGOSLAVIA	CZECHOSLOVAKIA	FRANCE
1964	SPAIN	SOVIET UNION	HUNGARY	DENMARK
1968	ITALY	YUGOSLAVIA	ENGLAND	SOVIET UNION
1972	WEST GERMANY	SOVIET UNION	BELGIUM	HUNGARY
1976	CZECHOSLOVAKIA	WEST GERMANY	HOLLAND	YUGOSLAVIA
1980	WEST GERMANY	BELGIUM	CZECHOSLOVAKIA	ITALY
1984	FRANCE	SPAIN	PORTUGAL/DENMARK	
1988	HOLLAND	SOVIET UNION	WEST GERMANY/ITALY	
1992	DENMARK	WEST GERMANY	HOLLAND/SWEDEN	

The Third Place match in 1980, when CZECHOSLOVAKIA beat ITALY
9-8 on penalties, was the last of its kind.

PREVIOUS WINNERS

	WON BY	LOCATION
1960	THE SOVIET UNION	FRANCE
1964	SPAIN	SPAIN
1968	ITALY	ITALY
1972	WEST GERMANY	BELGIUM
1976	CZECHOSLOVAKIA	YUGOSLAVIA
1980	WEST GERMANY	ITALY
1984	FRANCE	FRANCE
1988	HOLLAND	WEST GERMANY
1992	DENMARK	SWEDEN

CHIEF SCORERS IN THE QUALIFYING ROUND

GOALS	SCORERS
12	Davor Suker (Croatia)
10	Hristo Stoichkov (Bulgaria)
9	Jurgen Klinsmann (Germany)
7	Emil Kostadinov (Bulgaria), Hakan Sukur (Turkey)
6	Domingos (Portugal), Gianfranco Zola (Italy)
5	Patrik Berger (Czech Republic), Youri Djorkaeff (France), Igor Kolyvanov (Russia), Florin Raduciou (Rumania), Kim Vilfort (Denmark)
4	John Collins (Scotland), Michael Laudrup (Denmark), Marc Overmars (Holland), Dmitri Radchenko (Russia), Fabrizio Ravanelli (Italy), Manuel Rui Costa (Portugal), Christian Seedorf (Holland)
3	Krassimir Balakov (Bulgaria), Ronald De Boer (Holland), Scott Booth (Scotland), Drulak (Czech Republic), Figo (Portugal), Wim Jonk (Holland), Sergei Kiriakov (Russia), Ulf Kirsten (Germany), Patrick Kluivert (Holland), Vasili Kulkov (Russia), Marius Lacatus (Rumania), Andreas Moeller (Germany), Paulo Alves (Portugal), Joao V. Pinto (Portugal), Brian Roy (Holland), Julio Salinas (Spain), Horst Siegl (Czech Republic)

PREVIOUS TOURNAMENTS

Just as Jules Rimet conceived the FIFA World Cup, first played for in 1930, it was another Frenchmen, Henri Delauney, who conceived the European Championship, played every intervening four years.

1960

WON BY
THE SOVIET UNION IN FRANCE

Titled 'The European Nations Cup', a knock-out formula had been agreed on. Seventeen teams had entered, so it was necessary to play a decider between CZECHOSLOVAKIA and the IRISH REPUBLIC to see who should continue. After losing 2-0 in Dublin, CZECHOSLOVAKIA won the return match in Bratislava 4-0.

The draw for the first and quarter-final rounds was made during the 1958 World Cup. Both rounds were played on a 'home and away' basis.

FIRST ROUND

Victories for the Soviet Union against Hungary
(the first match in Moscow played before 100,572 people!)

France against Greece	Yugoslavia against Bulgaria
Spain against Poland	Czechoslovakia against Denmark
Austria against Norway	Rumania against Turkey
Portugal against East Germany	

QUARTER-FINALS

The SOVIET UNION were given a bye, since SPAIN refused to travel to Moscow because of Russian participation in the Spanish Civil War.

France defeated Austria
Czechoslovakia defeated Rumania
Yugoslavia defeated Portugal

SEMI-FINALS

The only non-Communist country, FRANCE, was chosen as the venue for the finals, but attendances proved disappointing. Both semi-finals were played on 6 July 1960.

Yugoslavia v France: YUGOSLAVIA came from 2-4 down to win 5-4 in Paris against FRANCE, who were without *Kopa*, *Fontaine* or *Piantoni*. *Jerkovic* was on outstanding form.

Soviet Union v Czechoslovakia: In Marseille in atrocious heat, the SOVIET UNION beat CZECHOSLOVAKIA 3-0, with *Lev Yashin* in the Soviet goal on inspiring form.

Czechoslovakia v France: The CZECHS, however, went on to finish third by beating the hosts, FRANCE, 2-0 - again in Marseille before a bare 9348 spectators.

FINAL

The final, in Paris, was played the following day. It saw the SOVIET UNION become the first champions, coming from behind to win 2-1 after extra time against YUGOSLAVIA. It also saw another brilliant performance by *Lev Yashin* with his eagle eye and his immense self-assurance.

FINAL

PARIS 10 July 1960 Att. 17,966

SOVIET UNION 2   **YUGOSLAVIA 1 a.e.t.**
(Metreveli 50,   (Galic 41)
Ponedelnik 113)

SOVIET UNION
Yashin
Tchekeli, Kroutilov
Voinov, Maslenkin, Netto
Metreveli, Ivanov, Ponedelnik, Bubukin, Meshki

YUGOSLAVIA
Vidinic
Durkovic, Jusufi
Zanetic, Miladinovic, Perusic
Sekularac, Jerkovic, Galic, Matus, Kostic

1964

WON BY SPAIN IN SPAIN

29 countries entered the second competition, whose finals were held in Spain.

SECOND ROUND

Spain beat Northern Ireland
Republic of Ireland beat Austria
Hungary beat East Germany
Denmark beat Albania *(who'd qualified thanks to a walk over, Greece refusing to play)*
Luxembourg beat Holland
Sweden beat Yugoslavia
Soviet Union beat Italy.

QUARTER-FINALS

Spain beat the Republic of Ireland
Hungary beat France
Denmark beat Luxembourg *(in a play-off after two drawn matches)*
Soviet Union beat Sweden

SEMI-FINALS

Hungary v Spain: HUNGARY forced extra time against SPAIN in Madrid, before *Amancio* scored to give the home side a 2-1 win.

Soviet Union v Denmark: The SOVIET UNION easily defeated the amateurs of DENMARK 3-0.

Third-place match: It was the turn of HUNGARY (who fielded six reserve players) to defeat DENMARK 3-1.

FINAL

SPAIN took the lead, only for the SOVIET UNION to reply a minute later. A dreary match affected by heavy rain seemed destined for extra time until 6 minutes before the end, when *Marcelino* scored with a superb diving header from a cross by *Pereda*.

The two outstanding players in the side were *Amancio*, a remarkable dribbler who could shoot with either foot, and *Luis Suarez*, an elegant midfield general who'd been European Footballer of the Year for 1960. *Suarez* then transferred to Internazionale of Milan from Barcelona; he'd recently guided them to victory in the 1964 European Cup.

FINAL

MADRID 21 JUNE 1964 Att. 120,000

SPAIN 2
(Pereda, Marcelino)

SOVIET UNION 1
(Khusainov)

SPAIN
Irabar

Rivilla, Calleja

Fuste, Olivella, Zoco

Amancio, Pereda, Marcelino, Suarez, Lapetra

SOVIET UNION
Yashin

Chustikov, Mudrik

Voronin, Shesternev, Anitchin

Chislenko, Ivanov, Ponedelnik, Kornalev, Khusainov

1968

WON BY ITALY IN ITALY

The 'European Nations Cup' competition became known as 'The European Championship'. With 31 countries entering, there were 8 groups. The winners moved through to the quarter-final stage, which was played on a knock-out basis.

QUARTER-FINALS

Italy beat Bulgaria 2-3 away and 2-0 at home
Soviet Union beat Hungary 0-2 away and 3-0 at home
England beat Spain 1-0 at home and 2-1 away *(England qualified by winning the British Home Championships for 1966/67 and 1967/68)*
Yugoslavia beat France 1-1 away and 5-2 at home

SEMI-FINALS

ITALY was chosen as the host country for the finals, and met the SOVIET UNION in one semi-final.

Italy v Soviet Union: The SOVIET UNION were without two key forwards in *Chislenko* and *Khurstliva*. Italy were captained by the tall *Giacinto Facchetti* as a commanding left-back, and played a strictly defensive game. The SOVIET UNION were unable to break through, and a goalless match was resolved by the toss of a coin!

England v Yugoslavia: In the other semi-final, the favourites, ENGLAND, lost 0-1 to YUGOSLAVIA in Florence after *Alan Mullery* was dismissed. The ten players (without *Hurst* and *Stiles*) struggled against the young Yugoslavians; only a minute before the end, they allowed the winger, *Dragan Dzajic*, to score. But ENGLAND beat the SOVIET UNION 2-0 in the third place match.

FINAL

Dzajic scored first. ITALY did not equalise until 9 minutes from time, when a free kick by *Angelo Domenghini* rocketed into the back of the net - even though the referee was ordering the Yugoslavian wall back. The final score remained 1-1.

REPLAY

Although the replay took place only two days later, YUGOSLAVIA were noticeably punished by making only one change, whereas ITALY made five. The goals came from *Luigi Riva* in the 12th minute and *Pietro Anastasi* in the 31st minute.

FINAL

ROME 8 June 1968 Att. 85,000

ITALY I	YUGOSLAVIA I a.e.t.
(Domenghini 81)	(Dzajic 40)

ITALY

Zoff

Burgnich, Facchetti

Ferrini, Guarneri, Castano

Domenghini, Juliano, Anastasi, Lodetti, Prati

YUGOSLAVIA

Pantelic

Fazlagic, Damjanovic

Pavlovic, Paunovic, Holcer

Petkovic, Acimovic, Musemic, Trivic, Dzajic

REPLAY

ROME 10 June 1968 Att. 50,000

ITALY 2	Yugoslavia 0
(Riva 12, Anastasi 31)	

ITALY

Z; B, F; Rosato, G, Salvadore; D, Mazzola, A, De Sisti, Riva

YUGOSLAVIA

P; F, D; P, P, H; Hosic, A, M, T, D

1972

WON BY
WEST GERMANY IN BELGIUM

All 32 nations entered, with each first-round group containing four teams.

QUARTER-FINALS

West Germany eliminated England 3-1 away and 0-0 at home
Belgium eliminated Italy 0-0 away and 2-1 at home
Hungary eliminated Rumania 1-1 at home and 2-2 away
Soviet Union eliminated Yugoslavia 0-0 away and 3-1 at home

West Germany v England: In beating a defensively-minded ENGLAND at
Wembley, WEST GERMANY revealed itself to be a class team. As
goalkeeper, *Sepp Maier* had shown himself to be a real lover of the 'big'
occasion. *Franz Beckenbauer* had up till then played as a midfield player
with defensive gifts. Now he moved back to become an attacking sweeper.
This tournament showed that he had an overall vision of the play which
enabled him to move speedily into positions where he could intercept
opposing attackers.

In midfield was the long-striding and graceful *Gunther Netzer*. Leading the
attack was *Gerd Muller*, one of the most lethal predators of his time. In
1970 he had become the first West German player to be elected European
Footballer of the Year.

SEMI-FINALS

In one semi-final, **Muller**'s 2 goals in the 2-1 defeat of the hosts,
BELGIUM, put WEST GERMANY through to meet the SOVIET UNION
who had defeated HUNGARY 1-0 in the other semi-final.

FINAL

The entire team maintained this outstanding form in the one-sided final.
They emphatically outplayed the SOVIET UNION, who were massively

indebted to *Rudakov*. *Muller*'s 2 goals in the final brought his total in the tournament to 11.

FINAL

BRUSSELS 18 June 1972 Att. 43,437

WEST GERMANY 3   **SOVIET UNION 0**

(Muller 43, Wimmer 48, Muller 53)

WEST GERMANY

Maier

Hottges, Schwarzenbeck, Beckenbauer, Breitner

Hoeness, Wimmer, Netzer

Heynckes, Muller, Kremer

SOVIET UNION

Rudakov

Dzodzuashvili, Khurtsilava, Kaplichny, Istomin

Troshkin, Kolotov, Baidachni

Konkov (Dolmatov), Banishevsky (Kozinkievits), Onishenko

1976

WON BY
CZECHOSLOVAKIA IN YUGOSLAVIA

Czechoslovakia had eliminated England *(the second consecutive time England were knocked out by the eventual winners).*
The Soviet Union had knocked out the Republic of Ireland.
Yugoslavia had knocked out Northern Ireland.
Spain had knocked out Scotland

QUARTER-FINALS

Czechoslovakia eliminated the Soviet Union 2-0 at home and 2-2 away
Holland eliminated Belgium 5-0 at home and 2-1 away
Yugoslavia eliminated Wales 2-0 at home an 1-1 away
West Germany eliminated Spain 1-1 away and 2-0 at home

SEMI-FINALS

These took place in Yugoslavia.

Czechoslovakia v Holland: CZECHOSLOVAKIA beat HOLLAND 3-1, scoring the last 2 goals during extra time, and dismissed thoughts of a rerun of the 1974 World Cup Final. *Johan Cruyff*, the best attacker of the era, had been voted European Footballer of the Year for 1971, 1973 and 1974. But even his lightning-fast reactions couldn't compensate for having two players sent off against a team who played an extra defender.

West Germany v Yugoslavia: The following day WEST GERMANY came from being 0-2 down at half-time to beat YUGOSLAVIA 4-2, although they could have been 0-5 down at the interval. The goals came from both the substitutes, *Heinz Flohe* and *Dieter Muller*. *Muller* scored a hat-trick - the last 2 of his goals coming in extra time.

The Third Place. Holland v Yugoslavia: HOLLAND (without *Cruyff* and *Neeskens* who were both suspended) defeated YUGOSLAVIA 3-2, also after extra time.

FINAL

The following day saw the unfancied CZECHOSLOVAKIA gain a 2-0 lead through goals from *Svehlik* and *Dobias*. But the Germans are never beaten, and came back with goals by *Dieter Muller* and *Holzenbein* against a tiring Czech defence - so that, as in both semi-finals, the final had to enter extra time.

The score remained 2-2 after 120 minutes. But unlike 1968, it was decided that there would be no replay in case of a draw. The result was decided for the first time by a penalty shoot-out, which CZECHOSLOVAKIA won 5-3.

FINAL

BELGRADE 20 June 1976 Att. 45,000

CZECHOSLOVAKIA 2 **WEST GERMANY 2 a.e.t.**
(Svehlik, Dobias)   (D. Muller, Holzenbein)
CZECHOSLOVAKIA
WON 5-3 ON PENALTIES)

CZECHOSLOVAKIA
Viktor
Pivarnik, Gogh
Dobias (Vesely), Capkovic, Ondrus
Masny, Panenka, Svehlik (Jurkemik), Moder, Nehoda

WEST GERMANY
Maier
Vogts, Schwarzenbeck, Beckenbauer, Dietz
Bonhof, Hoeness, Wimmer (Flohe), Beer (Bongartz)
D. Muller, Holzenbein

1980

WON BY WEST GERMANY IN ITALY

QUALIFIERS

The tournament was expanded for the sixth series. The final eight teams, however, weren't involved in a knockout round. Instead they were divided into two groups of four, with Italy, the host nation, being given automatic entry into the last eight.

> Group 1
> Czechoslovakia, West Germany, Holland, Greece

> Group 2
> Italy, England, Belgium, Spain

ENGLAND qualified at last, after having been eliminated from the previous tournaments by the eventual winners, WEST GERMANY in 1972 and CZECHOSLOVAKIA in 1976. Their most influential players were *Kevin Keegan*, an effervescent forward, and the graceful inside-forward *Trevor Brooking*. In 1977 *Keegan* had left Liverpool to play in Germany for Hamburg, and had been voted European Footballer of the Year for 1978 and 1979.

GROUP 1

WEST GERMANY beat CZECHOSLOVAKIA 1-0 and HOLLAND 3-2, before drawing a meaningless match 0-0 with Greece - who had lost 1-0 to HOLLAND and 3-1 to CZECHOSLOVAKIA. WEST GERMANY thus qualified for its third successive final.

GROUP 2

ENGLAND drew 1-1 with BELGIUM, and then lost 1-0 to ITALY, although they controlled most of the first half. Despite the absence of *Paolo Rossi*, who had been banned for involvement in a bribery scandal, *Giancarlo Antognoni* was in inspiring form in the midfield. The Italian goal came from *Marco Tardelli*, 10 minutes before the final whistle. It was a match disfigured by the use of tear gas against English fans, which, thanks to the wind, affected both sets of players.

The 2-1 victory against SPAIN thus became meaningless, but not the grim 0-0 draw between ITALY and BELGIUM, who'd defeated SPAIN 2-1 and qualified for the final.

Third Place. *Czechoslovakia v Italy*: CZECHOSLOVAKIA beat ITALY 9-8 on penalties, after the teams had drawn 1-1 in what must be regarded as one of the most sterile matches in the history of the entire competition.

FINAL

Appearing in its third consecutive final, WEST GERMANY's star was *Karl-Heinz Rummenigge*, a blond-haired winger who liked to surge in on goal and score himself. He would be voted European Footballer for 1980. But it was Hamburg's towering centre-forward, *Horst Hrubesch*, who scored twice, the second coming 2 minutes before the game seemed destined to enter extra time. WEST GERMANY thus became the first country to win the title twice.

FINAL

ROME 22 JUNE 1980 Att. 47,864

WEST GERMANY 2
(Hrubesch 40, Hrubesch 88)

BELGIUM 1
(Vandereycken 71 penalty)

WEST GERMANY
Schumacher
Kaltz, K.N. Forster, Stielike, Dietz
Briegel (Cullmann), Schuster, H. Muller
Rummenigge, Hrubesch, Allofs

BELGIUM
Pfaff
Gerets, Millecamp, Meeuws, Renquin
Van Moer, Cools, Vandereycken, Van der Elst
Mommens, Ceulemanns

1984

WON BY FRANCE IN FRANCE

For the second time the finals were held in France. They were won, appropriately, by France, who'd reached the semi-finals of the 1982 World Cup.

QUALIFIERS

France
Belgium *(eliminated Scotland)*
Portugal
Denmark *(eliminated England)*
Yugoslavia *(eliminated Wales)*
Rumania *(eliminated the world champions, Italy)*
West Germany *(eliminated Northern Ireland)*
Spain *(eliminated the Republic of Ireland; and, needing to win their last match by 11 clear goals to displace Holland, had beaten Malta 12-1!).*

GROUP 1

FRANCE headed Group 1 with 6 points, beating DENMARK 1-0 (during which *Alan Simonsen* had his leg broken), BELGIUM 5-0 and YUGOSLAVIA 3-2 (with *Michel Platini* scoring his second consecutive hat-trick).
DENMARK was second with 4 points from victories against YUGOSLAVIA 5-0 and BELGIUM 3-2.

GROUP 2

SPAIN headed Group 2 with 4 points from 1-1 draws against RUMANIA and PORTUGAL, and a 1-0 victory against WEST GERMANY.
PORTUGAL came second, also with 4 points after a 0-0 draw with WEST GERMANY and a 1-0 defeat of RUMANIA. During this game PORTUGAL had its star player, *Chalana*, stretchered off in the 17th minute.

SEMI-FINALS

France v Portugal: After cruising through the early games, FRANCE won a thrilling semi-final against PORTUGAL 3-2 after extra time.

Spain v Denmark: SPAIN defeated DENMARK 5-4 on penalties, after the score had been 1-1.

FINAL

Matters remained close until the 56th minute, when SPAIN's goalkeeper allowed a free kick by *Platini* to squeeze through his hands after he seemed to have hold of it. And SPAIN couldn't find an equaliser before its desperate attacks left space for FRANCE's *Bruno Bellone* to run through to score in the last minute.

It had been a wonderful, well-supported competition. FRANCE's triumph was due to its powerful midfield, and especially inspired by *Michel Platini* - probably the greatest French player of all time. A real specialist with free kicks, he loved to make telling runs into the attack. In mid-1982 he had been transferred from St Etienne to the Italian side of Juventus, and had just helped them to win the Italian championship. He'd been voted the top European Footballer for 1983.

FINAL

PARIS 27 June 1984 Att. 47,368

FRANCE 2   SPAIN 0
(Platini 56, Bellone 90)

FRANCE
Bats
Battiston (Amoros 72), Le Roux, Bossis, Domerque
Fernandez, Giresse, Tigana, Platini
Lacombe (Genghini 79), Bellone

SPAIN
Arconada
Urquiaga, Salva (Roberto 84), Camacho
Gallego, Senor, Francisco, Victor, Julio Alberto (Sarabia 76)
Santillana, Carrasco

1988

WON BY
HOLLAND IN WEST GERMANY

West Germany were selected to be hosts for the 1988 tournament, and given automatic entry to the final stages. The other 32 teams were split into seven groups, four groups of five countries and three groups of four countries.

QUALIFIERS

West Germany
Spain
Italy
Soviet Union
England *(eliminated Northern Ireland, gained an outstanding 4-1 win against Yugoslavia in Belgrade, and qualified with a 19-1 goal difference)*
Holland
Denmark *(eliminated Wales)*
Republic of Ireland *(eliminated a Scotland side that, in their penultimate game, gained victory in Sofia against the group leaders, Bulgaria. That brought delight in Dublin, since it was the first major championship that Ireland had qualified for.)*

GROUP 1

WEST GERMANY who in the first Group drew 1-1 with ITALY before going on to beat DENMARK 2-0 and SPAIN 2-0. ITALY beat SPAIN 1-0 and DENMARK 2-0 to finish second.

GROUP 2

ENGLAND lost 1-0 to a goal by *Ray Houghton* for Ireland in a game when *Pat Bonner* in IRELAND's goal was on outstanding form. And ENGLAND lost by 3-1 to both HOLLAND and the SOVIET UNION. Crucial to ENGLAND's sad performance was the attack of hepatitis which affected the form of *Gary Lineker*, the top scorer in the 1986 World Cup, who was now playing for Barcelona.

England v Holland: In this game there was a typical deep run by *Bryan Robson* who scored after playing a one-two with *Gary Lineker*. This brought the sides level, before HOLLAND's *Marco Van Basten* completed his hat-trick with two goals. *Van Basten's* second goal came after an increasingly shaky ENGLAND defence failed to deal with a free kick by *Arnie Muhren*.

England v the Soviet Union: The ENGLAND defence again proved fallible against the SOVIET UNION, allowing *Aleinikov* to score in the 3rd minute, and after *Tony Adams* had equalised in the 16th minute, permitting two further scores.

Holland v Ireland: On the same day HOLLAND (who'd lost 0-1 to the SOVIET UNION) played IRELAND. IRELAND had drawn 1-1 with the SOVIET UNION, the superb volley by *Ronnie Whelan* from a long throw by *Mick McCarthy* being answered after half-time by *Oleg Protasov*.

So another draw for IRELAND would be enough. The score was 0-0 at the interval, but then *Rinus Michels*, the Dutch manager, brought on an extra forward as substitute, and it was the goal by *Wim Kieft* that gave HOLLAND both precious points.

SEMI-FINALS

Holland v West Germany: HOLLAND gained its first victory over WEST GERMANY after 32 years. GERMANY had scored through *Lothar Matthaus* and HOLLAND through *Ronald Koeman* following dubious second-half penalty decisions. But in the 88th minute HOLLAND's incisive *Marco Van Basten* ran onto a defence-splitting pass by *Jan Wouters* to slide the ball home.

Soviet Union v Italy: The other match also turned out to be a bruising encounter. The SOVIET UNION won 2-0, although they had no fewer than seven players booked in previous encounters. In fact *Oleg Kuznetsov*, their key central defender, had his name taken as early as the 2nd minute!

Both goals came in the second half, the first in the 59th minute when *Kuznetsov* broke from defence and passed to *Litovchenko*, who stabbed the ball past the ITALIAN goalkeeper, *Walter Zenga*. The second goal came two minutes later when *Protasov* struck home after a race down the left flank by *Zavarov*, the man of the match. The ITALIANS were disconsolate; although one of the bright stars on the pitch was the new left-back, *Paolo Maldini*, who was not yet 20.

But it was the SOVIET UNION who progressed to yet another European Championship final, full of confidence since they had already beaten HOLLAND 1-0.

FINAL

However, at the heart of the SOVIET defence they would lack *Kuznetsov*, who was out through suspension - and it showed. This time, with *Frank Rijkaard* playing as sweeper in front of, rather than behind, HOLLAND's defence, the SOVIET UNION were comprehensively outplayed.

Ruud Gullit, elected European Footballer of 1987, scored the first goal with a powerful header after 32 minutes. And 8 minutes after half-time came a truly memorable goal that must rank with the best ever scored. It came from the second Dutchman who had joined A. C. Milan in 1987, *Marco Van Basten*. Collecting a long cross from *Arnold Muhren*. who had once played for Ipswich Town, he smashed in a second from the acutest angle. No wonder he was elected the outstanding European footballer of the year. In the 59th minute HOLLAND's goalkeeper *Hans Van Breukelen* saved a penalty he himself had given away.

There were very few who couldn't agree that HOLLAND had been worthy winners, the first time they had won a major championship.

FINAL

MUNICH 25 June 1988 Att. 72,308

HOLLAND 2   **SOVIET UNION 0**
(Gullit 33, Van Basten 54)

HOLLAND
Van Breukelen
Van Aerle, Rijkaard, Koeman R., Van Tiggelen
Wouters, Vanenburg, Muhren, Koeman E.
Gullit, Van Basten

SOVIET UNION
Dassaev
Demianenko, Gotsmanov (Baltacha), Khidiatullin, Aleinikov
Mikhailichenko, Zavarov, Litovchenko
Protasov (Pasulko), Rats, Belanov

1992

WON BY DENMARK IN SWEDEN

QUALIFIERS

Sweden *(the hosts)*
England *(knocked out the Republic of Ireland)*
France *(the first country to qualify with a 100 per cent record)*
Denmark *(who replaced the talented Yugoslavia side, banished due to the
    civil war; both knocked out Northern Ireland)*
West Germany *(knocked out Wales)*
Holland
Commonwealth of Independent States - CIS *(formerly Soviet Union)*
Scotland *(there for the first time)*

GROUP I

France v Sweden: The opening game pitted FRANCE against SWEDEN
in Stockholm. Goals were expected from *Jean-Pierre Papin*, who'd been
voted European Footballer of the Year for 1991, and *Eric Cantona* who'd
just helped Leeds United win the England title.

SWEDEN, however, gained a 1-1 draw; a bullet header by the centre-back
Jan Eriksson was answered by a glorious goal from *Papin*. Collecting a
crossfield pass from *Christian Perez*, he outpaced the defenders and, from the
right, struck a shot past *Thomas Ravelli* in SWEDEN's goal. But FRANCE
should have been awarded a penalty when *Papin* was clearly pulled down in
the area by *Eriksson*.

England v Denmark: There was a draw in the other match. But this time it
was goalless, since ENGLAND was unable to break down DENMARK's
defence. In fact *John Jensen* came closest to scoring when he struck an
upright. ENGLAND clearly missed the goal-making flair of players such as
Paul Gascoigne - their inspiration in 1990 - and *John Barnes*. *Gascoigne*
suffered a serious injury a year earlier, and *Barnes* was injured just before the
start of the tournament. ENGLAND had been forced to enter the
tournament without key defenders such as *Mark Wright*, another star in the

World Cup, *Rob Jones*, the exciting new right-back, and *Gary Stevens*, who'd been injured.

France v England: FRANCE made several changes when they played ENGLAND, who'd beaten them 2-0 at Wembley in February. They left out the creative *Perez* and, astonishingly, packed the midfield with defensive players: the team that preached and showed splendid flair preferring to play defensively! The consequence was 90 minutes of tedium, with FRANCE cynically anticipating a victory in the third match against DENMARK.

Minor injuries had been plentiful during the competition, but it was a vicious head-butt by *Basile Boli*, unseen by the referee, that gave *Stuart Pearce* a cut on the right cheek. And with FRANCE packing its midfield, the closest ENGLAND came to scoring was when *Pearce* drove a ferocious free kick onto the underside of the bar, and when *Alan Shearer* just failed to slide home a pass from *Andy Sinton*.

So, with two goalless draws, ENGLAND simply had to win its next match, in Stockholm, against SWEDEN. They'd defeated DENMARK 1-0 the same evening, thanks to a goal by *Brolin* in the 59th minute, so they had 3 points.

England v Sweden: ENGLAND made an encouraging start: in the 4th minute *David Platt* knocked home a cross from *Gary Lineker*. Joy for ENGLAND's travelling supporters, but that crucial second goal never materialised. Four chances weren't taken. And ENGLAND were extremely lucky when *David Batty*, playing at right-back, made a rash challenge on *Brolin*. It was a clear penalty to everyone except the Portuguese referee.

Matters changed at half-time, however, when SWEDEN took off *Anders Limpar* and substituted another forward, *Johnny Ekstroem*, to put added pressure on ENGLAND's defence. The tactic worked handsomely. *Eriksson* scored in the 52nd minute, and the midfield now being run by *Jonas Thern* and *Stefan Schwarz*, the ENGLAND manager, Graham Taylor, controversially substituted his captain *Gary Lineker* ten minutes later. ENGLAND were now totally at sea without the mastery of the man who'd scored 48 international goals. In the 82nd minute *Brolin* finished off a delightful one-two with *Martin Dahlin* to score the decisive goal.

Denmark v France: In the other game, DENMARK beat FRANCE 2-1. *Henrik Larsen* provided a great start, scoring in the 8th minute after he knocked in a cross from *Fleming Poulsen*. France wasn't able to equalise until the prolific *Papin* scored from a 20-metre drive from the left, after skilful work on the right by *Cantona*. But it was the Danes who had more of the play and scored the winner: the substitute *Lars Elstrup* slotted the ball home from a cross by *Fleming Poulsen*. It came as no surprise when *Michel Platini* promptly resigned as FRANCE's manager.

GROUP 2

This looked far the stronger, with all four teams having qualified for the 1990 finals. WEST GERMANY had been the victor then, but HOLLAND had won the previous European Championship in 1988, beating the SOVIET UNION, and again had *Rinus Michels* in charge. The SOVIET UNION was now competing as the COMMONWEALTH OF INDEPENDENT STATES (CIS), and the fourth team was SCOTLAND, who'd qualified for the first time.

In the past SCOTLAND's talent for making crass blunders against supposedly weaker teams was legendary. This time, as manager *Andy Roxburgh* pointed out, it was *they* who were the minnows. But luck was not with them in their opening game against HOLLAND.

Scotland v Holland: *Richard Gough* played outstandingly in the centre of the defence, and a draw against the team favoured by most people looked a distinct possibility. That is, until the 77th minute: *Ruud Gullit* passed to *Marco Van Basten* who passed to *Frank Rijkaard*, whose header over the defence was collected by *Dennis Bergkamp* - who poked home the only goal of the match.

Germany v CIS: The other match was an evenly-fought but grimmer contest. GERMANY lost its captain, *Rudi Voller*, with a broken arm at half-time. (*Lothar Mattheus* had been injured before the start of the tournament). The world champions, GERMANY, eventually went behind to a penalty scored by *Igor Dobrovolski* in the 63rd minute after he'd been pulled down in the area by *Stefan Reuter*. *Dmitri Kharin* in the CIS goal was on inspiring form, and GERMANY were all set to join SCOTLAND with no points. Then in the 90th minute a swerving free-kick by *Thomas*

Haessler passed over *Kharin's* right shoulder into the net to give GERMANY 2 points.

Holland v CIS: HOLLAND and the CIS then drew 0-0. *Dmitri Kharin* again had an outstanding match, although late in the second half *Marco Van Basten* had a vital goal mistakenly ruled offside.

Scotland v Germany: In its splendid match against GERMANY, SCOTLAND were extremely unlucky not to achieve at least a draw. It was full of chances at both ends, but in the 28th minute SCOTLAND's defence failed to control *Jurgen Klinsmann*. His pass to *Karlheinz Riedle* was followed by a thunderous shot. Just a minute into the second half, GERMANY scored another goal as a cross from *Stefan Effenberg* which was deflected past *Andy Goram*.

Scotland v CIS: After gaining no points from two close games, SCOTLAND then ruined any CIS hopes of reaching the semi-finals by scoring twice in the first 17 minutes, thanks to shots by *Paul McStay* and *Brian McClair*. With the CIS incapable of responding, SCOTLAND went 3-0 up in the 83rd minute when *Gary McAllister* struck home a penalty after *Pat Nevin* was pulled down. The Scots could return home with their heads held high.

Holland v Germany: The other match in Gothenburg, was packed with Dutch supporters fervid with their hatred of GERMANY. HOLLAND pushed *Frank Rijkaard* into midfield and overwhelmed a GERMAN team who had lost *Buchwald* and *Reuter* from their defence after the game against SCOTLAND. In only the 2nd minute, *Rijkaard* headed *Ronald Koeman's* free kick into the opposing net: in the 14th minute *Richard Witschge* struck a left-footed shot just inside the post. Although *Klinsmann* scored for GERMANY, in the 71st minute *Dennis Bergkamp* slid home a cross by *Aron Winter* to make the final score 3-1.

SEMI-FINALS

Sweden v Germany: In the first of these, SWEDEN faced a GERMANY who knew they would have to improve substantially on their previous performances. With both *Buchwald* and *Reuter* back, they did. In the 10th minute *Haessler* curled a free kick high into SWEDEN's net, with *Ravelli* not being able to make a move: in the 58th minute they went further ahead when *Riedle* struck home after a cross by *Matthias Sammer*. *Brolin* converted a penalty, but *Riedle* scored a third goal in the 88th minute. And although *Kennet Andersson* scored a minute later, GERMANY ran out as 3-2 winners.

It seemed that another GERMANY-versus-HOLLAND confrontation was inevitable, the third battle in consecutive tournaments between these arch-rivals. But along came DENMARK to spoil the story.

Denmark v Holland: In the 5th minute *Henrik Larsen* headed home a perfect cross from *Brian Laudrup*. DENMARK were having most of the play, so it came as a surprise when *Peter Schmeichel* went down to his right too late to stop a shot by *Dennis Bergkamp*, who drove home a skilful header by *Frank Rijkaard*. In the 32nd minute DENMARK regained their advantage as *Larsen* drove the ball home.

As in 1988, HOLLAND's answer was to bring on *Wim Kieft* at half-time. But the Dutch forced few opportunities and it wasn't until the 85th minute that *Rijkaard* was able to score from a corner. As extra time progressed, HOLLAND appeared to grow more powerful, but failed to score. The match had to be decided on a penalty shoot-out: the only miss came when *Marco Van Basten*'s shot was saved by an inspired *Peter Schmeichel*, but *Kim Christofte* scored the fifth and decisive Danish penalty.

FINAL

As in 1976, WEST GERMANY finished as finalists since in the semi-final HOLLAND had drawn the supposedly easier opponents. But now it would be GERMANY's turn to experience defeat. *Schmeichel* was again in inspired form, snatching the ball off the head of *Klinsmann* as early as the 4th minute. But in the 18th minute came true drama. *Kim Vilfort* took the ball off *Brehme* and back-heeled it for the midfielder *John Jensen*, to score with a twenty-yard drive. And, with the skilful DENMARK increasingly controlling the game against a spoiling GERMANY, the result came as no surprise. With 12 minutes remaining, midfielder *Kim Vilfort* scored, running on to a header from substitute *Claus Christiansen* to whip in a low drive with his left foot.

It had been a true fairy-tale ending after one of the largest upsets in international football. DENMARK - a last-minute substitute for the talented YUGOSLAVIA - emerged as victors. The Danes knew definitely they would be taking part only a week before the first game. But they had shown themselves to be a skilful side in 1984 and the World Cup of 1986. And since the finals would be played in nearby Sweden, they were guaranteed massive support.

FINAL

GOTHENBURG 26 June 1992 Att. 37,800

DENMARK 2   **GERMANY 0**
(Jensen 18, Vilfort 78)

DENMARK
Schmeichel
Sivebaeck (Christiansen 65), Nielsen K., Olsen, Piechnik
Christofte, Jensen, Larsen, Vilfort
Laudrup, Poulsen

GERMANY
Illgner
Reuter, Kohler, Helmer, Buchwald, Brehme
Haessler, Sammer (Doll 46), Effenberg (Thom 81)
Klinsmann, Riedle

INDEX

Bulgaria...16
Croatia 18
Czech Republic 20
Denmark...22
England...24
France 26
Germany...28
Holland...30
Italy 32
Players..48
Portugal 34
Previous Tournaments:
    1960 72
    1964 74
    1968 76
    1972 78
    1976 80
    1980 82
    1984 84
    1988 86
    1992 90
Qualifying Round..12
Rumania 36
Russia 38
Scotland 40
Spain...42
Switzerland 44
Turkey..46